"PAST MASTER"

Thoughts on Teaching and the Teaching Life

Peter Gow

LICENSING AND COPYRIGHT

"PAST MASTER" is copyright by Peter Gow ©2020 and licensed for publication by One Schoolhouse under a Creative Commons Attribution–NonCommercial–ShareAlike 4.0 International License. You are free to:
- ✓ **Share**—copy and redistribute the material in any medium or format
- ✓ **Adapt**—remix, transform, and build upon the material Under the following terms:
- ✓ **Attribution**—You must give appropriate credit, provide a link to the license, and indicate if changes were made. You may do so in any reasonable manner, but not in any way that suggests the licensor endorses you or your use.
- ✓ **NonCommercial**—You may not use the material for commercial purposes.
- ✓ **ShareAlike**—If you remix, transform, or build upon the material, you must distribute your contributions under the same license as the original.

The licensor cannot revoke these freedoms as long as you follow the license terms.

2020

.epub ISBN 978-1-7342479-0-9
.pdf ISBN 978-1-7342479-4-7
.mobi ISBN 978-1-7342479-5-4
Paperback ISBN 978-1-7342479-6-1

"PAST MASTER"

Thoughts on Teaching and the Teaching Life

by Peter Gow

One Schoolhouse
1342 Florida Avenue NW
Washington, DC 20009

ABOUT THE AUTHOR

Peter Gow (1950–) has been a teacher and an administrator in independent schools for over 40 years. He grew up on the campus of The Gow School and graduated from Nichols School in Buffalo, New York, before attending Yale and graduate school at Brown and Rhode Island College. He taught at The Gow School, Providence Country Day School, The Fessenden School, and Beaver Country Day School. He was a founding board member and then executive director of the Independent Curriculum Group and joined One Schoolhouse as Independent Curriculum Resource Director when the ICG merged with One Schoolhouse. Peter has written, consulted, and presented for schools and national educational organizations in the United States and Canada.

"PAST MASTER"
TABLE OF CONTENTS

PROLOGUE   1

MY JOURNEY   5
Perspective by Sean Raymond
1   TOWARD A NEW JERUSALEM?   5
2   LITERACY AND LUCK   8
3   MY FATHER'S SCHOOL—JUST FOR ME   10

WHY TEACH?   13
Perspective by Josie Holford
4   WHAT MAKES GREAT TEACHERS—AND WHAT ATTRACTS THEM TO SCHOOLS?   14
5   RESTITUTIONAL TEACHING: A THOUGHT ON WHY WE (OR AT LEAST SOME OF US MAY) TEACH   17
6   PAYING IT FORWARD: FURTHER THOUGHTS ON WHY WE (OR AT LEAST SOME OF US MAY) TEACH   19

EDUCATION, FROM THE OUTSIDE LOOKING IN   24
Perspective by Debi Ellman
7   YOUR FATHER'S (AND GRANDPARENTS') TEACHERS—A MEASURED APPRECIATION   25
8   THE PEOPLE OF MY VILLAGE   29
9   THE ORIGINAL DISRUPTOR: A CAUTIONARY REFLECTION ON DEAD POETS SOCIETY   31
10   EDU-PORN   34

TABLE OF CONTENTS

FINDING THE TEACHERS WE NEED   37
Perspective by Greg Martin
11   HAS YOUR SCHOOL DONE ITS "HIRING SELF-STUDY" YET?   38
12   "EMPLOYMENT AT" SCHOOL WEBPAGES   40
13   RECRUITING STRATEGIES   42
14   TWELVE MAXIMS FOR HIRING AND SUSTAINING TEACHERS   45

SUPPORTING TEACHERS   50
Perspective by Richard Kassissieh
15   A LETTER TO NEW TEACHERS   51
16   INDUCTION AND ORIENTATION FOR NEW TEACHERS   55
17   A CULTURE OF MENTORSHIP   57
18   FEEDBACK FOR NEW TEACHERS   59
19   MAKING TEACHERS   61
20   TEACHING STANDARDS   64

THE TEACHING LIFE   68
Perspective by Elise London
21   THE ALL-TERRAIN TEACHER   69
22   WHATEVER OUR PASSIONS, THERE IS A TIME TO BE STILL AND LISTEN   72
23   DEFINING, THEN SERVING, THE WHOLE CHILD   76
24   BUSY-NESS   78
25   SITTING DOWN TO TURKEY IN DISCOMFORT WITH MY PRIVILEGE   81
26   ANNALS OF TEACHING: BEING WRONG   84
27   ANNALS OF TEACHING: ON NIGHTMARES   86
28   NARRATIVE COMMENTS, GRADES, AND SCHOOLS   89

WANTING MORE FROM OUR WORK   92
Perspective by Thomas Mueller
29   MIDDLE MANAGEMENT—A NEW VISION   93
30   A NEW ERA FOR DEPARTMENT HEADS— PART I   96
31   A NEW ERA FOR DEPARTMENT HEADS— PART II   98

TEACHING IN PERILOUS TIMES   104
Perspective by Rebecca Yacono
32   *LOCKDOWN!*   104
33   SLOW-GRADING TEACHERS: CANARIES IN OUR COAL MINES   107

34   TOUGH TIMES: "PROFESSIONAL DEVELOPMENT AS R&D" 110

IN THE CLASSROOM 113
Perspective by Neal Keesee

35   "WHEN WILL I EVER NEED THIS?"—FIGURING OUT HOW TO TEACH WHAT MATTERS 115
36   TEACHING WRITING 117
37   MEMORY—IT'S A GOOD THING 120
38   CONTENT IN THE 21ST CENTURY 122
39   THE UNTAPPED POWER OF PROTOCOLS 124
40   FAILURE STUDIES 127
41   TECHNOLOGY, AND THEN SOME 130
42   SNOW DAY THOUGHTS FOR EDUCATORS—AND PARENTS, TOO 132

THE CULTURE OF TEACHING 136
Perspective by Jonathan Martin

43   TREATING TEACHERS LIKE GROWN-UPS 137
44   TEACHERS AND CHANGE—PART I 138
45   TEACHERS AND CHANGE—PART II 141
46   BANTER AND SCHOOL CULTURE 146
47   JOB DESCRIPTIONS 150
48   PARENT–TEACHER EVENTS 154
49   HOLIDAY GREETINGS: FAMILY STYLE! 157

ESPECIALLY FOR INDEPENDENT SCHOOL TEACHERS 160
Perspective by John Gulla

50   I AM AN INDEPENDENT SCHOOL TEACHER—WHY? 161
51   SOME THOUGHTS AND RESOURCES ON INDEPENDENT SCHOOL TEACHING 163
52   INDEPENDENT SCHOOLS, INDEPENDENT TEACHERS: FREEDOM AND RESPONSIBILITY 166

THE EPILOGUES 169
Perspective by Catherine Conover

53   THE LAST POST FOR MY FATHER 169
54   ON THE DEATH OF A TEACHER 172

PROLOGUE

The title of this book is ironic, more than you know.

The first school I worked at—beginning as part of the maintenance crew, then as a painter, then a development office rookie, and at last as a teacher and coach—still clung to the antiquated and now questionable usage of teachers as "masters." You can be sure that when I first stepped into my own classroom in 1975, I was a master of nothing: not of my own nerves, not of how to teach my subject matter, not of Arts. To have called myself a master then would have been a travesty, and I shamefacedly knew it. But in a world that even then (it wasn't all sex, drugs, and rock'n'roll, you know) still venerated headmasters and headmistresses and even senior masters, this was still current terminology. I spent a year trying to master some aspect of it, any aspect at all—to what avail only my students could tell you.

I was never so happy as when I soon found myself in schools where I was just a teacher, which of course meant that I was mostly a learner, spending the next 40 or so years trying to figure it all out. Along the way I had enough external validation to keep me at it, even as I discovered the manifold joys of working with students, with colleagues, and, in my final school, in a community explicitly dedicated to exploring how to do it all better. I was never called a master again, and that's just fine with me. That era seems now to have passed. By the time I closed up my last office, I had held enough "jobs" that I could almost have been called a jack of all trades in an independent school, and I hope I was at least competent at most of them. But was I a "master" of any of them? Who knows?

But I discovered, relatively late in life, that I enjoyed writing about schools and about teaching, and the era of the blog and the Ning gave me platforms to practice. I wanted, I guess, to explain myself (sometimes more to myself than to anyone else, and writing helps me still in that regard), and to run some ideas up a figurative flagpole as, in the first decade of this century, schools found themselves facing challenge after challenge and having the chance, if not the necessity, thrust in their faces of considering whether and how to incorporate any droplets of the "21st-century education" tidal wave of new ideas and understandings about teaching and learning.

I kept at it, maintaining over time a bunch of blogs of my own and guesting here and there. In my mind's ear I heard my ideas as theorems and theories posited before an audience, but in retrospect I may have sounded a bit absolutist and maybe even strident, far more often than I had intended. If I didn't consider myself a "master" of much, I may have come across as pretending to be one. For this I apologize.

Back when I first started writing these posts, Anthony Cody in *Education Week* offered up a kind of Hippocratic Oath for teachers, and I still find its self-consciously lofty language kind of moving. One point sticks with me:

> *I will work with my colleagues to inspire one another to achieve excellence. I will not be ashamed to say "I know not," nor will I fail to call in my colleagues when the skills of another are needed to help my students.*

Having been fortunate enough to work with brilliant colleagues in my schools and to have gotten to know a host of brilliant colleagues around the industry, I offer up the essays that follow as inspiration, as provocation, as perspective, but most of all as one old teacher's simultaneous cry for help and offer of assistance as we work together to make education better for all students in all kinds of schools, everywhere.

PROLOGUE

If I get it wrong, please tell me. As Robert Burns tells us in other words, we don't always know when "we know not," and it would be a gift to see this in ourselves.

I also note, with some dismay, that topics about which I was writing a decade and more ago remain disappointingly current today. Issues around leadership, teacher development, school culture, and even curriculum and instruction that seemed on the cusp of general correction back in the day seem still to exist in and even characterize many schools in 2020. Much of what we have learned about making learning stick and designing experiences that are more relevant, more salubrious, and more engaging seems not to have permeated every school so far, with marketplace (and marke*ting*) anxieties perhaps acting as a brake on real innovation and more importantly on turning ideals into action.

Perhaps the persistence of some of these issues can be attributed to economic uncertainty. In the autumn of 2008 the shoe had dropped; in the winter of 2020 it seems to be dangling by a frayed lace.

"Past Master" with its ironic title is offered, then, as a booster shot for educators and schools in need of a little more of the courage of their own convictions.

NOTES ON THE TEXT: These essays first appeared as free-standing blog posts here and there. In preparing this e-book I have made some editorial updates and corrections so that I can stand by what I wrote as my truth in 2020. The original sources are cited after each essay, and the original posts are still available online as of this writing.

St. Basalt's School has been my generic name for "any independent school" for years.

I subscribe, perhaps inconsistently, to the use of gender-free general pronouns, including the singular "they" and "themself." These are real things these days, even if seasoned Grammar Police may be stroking their nightsticks in consternation. But be prepared.

MY JOURNEY

Perspective by Sean Raymond, Assistant Head of School and Academic Dean, York School

One of my favorite yoga teachers always ends class by recognizing her teachers. "I want to thank my teacher, and my teacher's teachers, and the teachers of those teachers. We exist in a lineage of wisdom and love." I have long been grateful for the writings of Peter Gow, with their pedigree of whimsy and wisdom. In the passages that follow, we experience his sense of connectedness through the poetry of Blake, the blessing of literacy from 4th grade to the convalescent home, and delightful reflections on his father's didactic ways. For these, I wish to thank Peter's teachers, and his teachers' teachers, and the teachers of those teachers.

1 TOWARD A NEW JERUSALEM?

I've long been puzzled by some of the weirder aspects of William Blake's poem "Jerusalem." What was this man talking about, imagining Jesus bopping around England, touching down on a verdant hill here and a sooty factory there? Having taught the poem on occasion, I have pondered it both as an example of English Romanticism and as what it has become (for better or for worse, we admit): the anthem of a particular vision, or version, of England.

Scholars have commented extensively on the role that Blake's rather off-beat and romantic Christian—gnostic, if you will—faith played in his life and poetry, but as I have continued to ponder "Jerusalem"—some days I can't get the tune of the hymn version out of my head—I have realized that what Blake *really* believed in was not God, or Christ, but England. Why else would he express the notion that England had been, and could be, a Promised Land, even with its "dark Satanic mills"? A part of Blake must have been consumed by a romantic, perfectionist vision not of an England as a Holy Land based on testamentary principles but rather as a green and pleasant Utopia, based on the humble, humane values and virtues that the word "pleasant" shouts so loudly by its own almost absurd modesty; you'd mark a student down who used "pleasant" in an essay to describe anything so important.

I think I know what Blake was getting at. Social psychologists, evangelicals, sports fans, and athletes know it, too. It's that feeling of oneness with a corporate whole—a congregation, a filled stadium, the bench, even a family group—when some extraordinary, affirming, positive event (a great sermon, a last-minute goal, an expression of warmth and love from great-grandmother, even a choir singing "Jerusalem" in exquisite harmony) draws the group together in a moment of transcendent community and joy. (I'll go so far as to suggest that the U.S. men's ice hockey victory over the Soviet Union in the 1980 Olympics may have been the largest expression of this feeling in my lifetime.)

For me, as a non-religious person in whom the spirit occasionally stirs, this feeling is how I define "god," or at least a godly intention for humankind: the intention of peace and comity that is manifest as Jesus delivers the Sermon on the Mount. I've always been moved by the idea that those folks discovered that with a little generosity of spirit, the loaf of Wonder Bread and half-can of tuna fish (thank you, forgotten comedian from whom I have borrowed this line) to which the crowd initially copped could expand, when the people turned from protecting their own stuff to sharing it with others, into a satisfying meal for a multitude. This belief in the goodness and fairness of one's fellows is the root of my personal hope for a New Jerusalem, for utopia.

I've spent most of my life in schools, and I'm slowly coming to define the tenets of my true faith.

I believe in school the way Blake, amid the squalor of the Industrial Revolution, believed in England.

I believe that any school—with an optimistic, generous mission and clear, affirming, pro-human values—and the right students and the right faculty and the right leadership, can be what Blake dreamt of for England: Jerusalem, or at least a promised land. I love that feeling of being almost (and sometimes not just almost) weepy with joy and gratitude at Commencement and that sense of complete sharing that would come over me in those occasional faculty meetings where everyone was in agreement about something wonderful. I loved watching my own kids walk off down the hall each morning as we arrived in the building. My spirit has been renewed by those random conversations with students in which all parties—old and young—suddenly drill down to some important truths about one another and about their experience of learning and life. I'm physically and emotionally thrilled when I go back to the words of the most idealistic of school founders and find eternal truths about student-centered education, and I have been equally thrilled when colleagues have voiced their own faith in similar truths.

What better vision can a school aspire to than being, in its way, "a green and pleasant land"? To be a place where growth is nourished and in which growing beings flourish, and to be a place where kindness and decency prevail? That's an ideal school. That's a paradise worthy of faith and hope, and love.

Why can't every school be Jerusalem, and why shouldn't I believe in this?

Not Your Father's School, April 6, 2018

2 LITERACY AND LUCK

I'm a lucky man.

Upon occasion I do reflect in my old age on the heaps of cultural and social capital I carry around, or rather that carry me around, elevated perhaps above my true existential worth by flukes of race and gender and the socioeconomic accident of birth.

But I'm also lucky because I am literate, (again accidentally) born into a family who happens to put value on that capacity, and the social and cultural capital that come with it, and who have put lives' worth of effort into extending this bounty to others. I'm lucky to be the parent of kids who value literacy, too, and who seem inclined to do something about paying it forward.

A few years back I had a crazy idea, to turn the whole of what we now generally call fourth grade into an extravaganza of reading, all day, every day, gently guided by teacher-coaches and literacy and reading specialists. The idea was to tidy up deficits and get kids into the habit of exploring their interests through the wonders of the written word. I wouldn't be fussy — comic books, graphic novels, kid lit, are all okay with me, and what better way into STE(A)M-y subjects than through books (any genres!) and other publications on art, mathematics, engineering, and science; and I'm also okay with e-readers and texts like blogs or even short-form social media read on line. By the time the kids were ready for grade five, they'd all be readers, their difficulties identified and in remediation, their interests sparked.

I'm still waiting for a school to call me and say they've taken up the [challenge I issued in *Education Week* on this topic](), but I still have hopes, and so apparently does one of my own kids.

The kid in question messaged me from college the other night (he's a senior) and sent me a link to an article of [Laurene Powell Jobs's new school-founding initiative](#) along with some thoughts:

"Revive your 4th grade reading plan? High school is far too late to make an impactful change, unfortunately."

"If you care about fundamentals, start early. ...How often does one read under supervision? Kids go home, but do we know they're reading? A classroom centered around books could ensure that nobody passes through without being literate, which is of foundational importance to all other fields."

And later: "Literacy is the magic bullet that cures everything."

I haven't given my fourth-grade idea much though lately, but I think about reading and writing all the time.

I thought about it last weekend when I realized that each of the home health caregivers looking after my aging stepmother finishes her shift by writing out, in long-hand on the pages of a spiral notebook, a lengthy report on the previous hours. Quite possibly, over the course of a week, these amazing people do more writing than I do, and their writing has a life-or-death significance that their elementary school teachers never thought about and that wasn't, probably, a big part of their training.

But there it is. Along with a pretty good-sized stack of spiral notebooks about how to keep another human being alive and comfortable.

So next time I'm feeling lucky, I will add literacy to my list of good fortunes, and I urge readers(!) to do the same. And not just about your and my own literacy, but the vast and plentiful literacies of the world around us, literacies that have brought us pleasure, safety, progress, and even the gadgets upon which I write and you read.

Appreciate the capacity that gives caregivers a tool for sharing vital information and that gives me a chance to text with a kid away at college who cherishes literacy, too.

Not Your Father's School, September 16, 2015

3   MY FATHER'S SCHOOL—JUST FOR ME

For a long time after my father died two and a half years ago, I would occasionally have dreams in which he was present in the world of the dream but not present in my direct experience in the dream. He was there, but not *right* there. I imagine this is a not-uncommon experience.

More recently, however, he has made appearances, although there hasn't been much communication that I recall between dream-Pop and dream-me. But one of these dreams awakened me to something I've been thinking about: *Things my father made sure I knew when I was a kid.*

For example, my father wasn't always entirely impressed by my own teachers, and on occasion he would do the intellectual equivalent of strapping explosives to me before sending me off for some interaction with one of them. Once it was to teach me the term "aeger," which in British university usage is a medical excuse from something. (How did he know this? Beats me. It's the kind of thing he liked knowing.) I handed some poor teacher a note requesting an aeger from athletics, prompting a request for an explanation. When I gave the explanation, the teacher was certain I was being disrespectful and flippant, which perhaps to an extent I was, and before the episode had ended, I had been required to write a note of apology to the teacher.

In time I had to write further notes of apology to this same teacher over points of literary interpretation—once because I had requested adjudication by *Bartlett*'s over the exact wording of a quotation and once because I had suggested that "realms of gold" extended not just to the content of books but to the gold lettering on the cover of *Chapman's Homer*; the copy at my grandmother's house had gold lettering and gold leaf on the page edges. In each case my father had somehow spurred my thinking, whether or not it was intended to annoy my revered but touchy English teacher. But I have my suspicions.

My father made sure to fill my head with arcane vocabulary, odd facts, and occasional blatant untruths. (When finally I could not avoid eating fish, I was pleased to discover that the family medical condition that meant "if Gows eat fish, they will die" apparently hadn't infected me. It hadn't occurred to me that tuna fish sandwiches, which Pop ate regularly, are actually made from, er, fish.) This out-of-the-way knowledge has given me considerable private amusement over the years, and I've tried to pass some of it along to my own children and to my students; many of them can still tell you that "Hope, Arkansas, is the Watermelon Capital of the World," a factoid I learned from my father before anyone outside of Hope had ever heard of Bill Clinton.

We also spent quite a lot of time as a family looking at art, either at the Albright-Knox in Buffalo with its stunning and often puzzling collection of Modern work, or at the local "art dealer," who made most of his money selling frames but occasionally moved a modest Picasso print or a small work by a contemporary painter. There were also white-covered Skira art books around the house to supplement what we could see in person.

There were things that my father couldn't or didn't want to teach me but made sure that someone else did. For example, Curt Fraser, the school maintenance man—the one and only at the time, for a seventy-acre campus with a dozen buildings—taught me how to drive a tractor when I was eleven, and I still drive a stick-shift car. Alas, there has been no Curt to teach my children, who are automatic-only; their father regrettably lacks the patience to teach them. Incidentally that tractor, still in use at the school, actually figured in my most recent dream involving my father, the dream that inspired this post.

Over the last few days, as Father's Day approaches, my Facebook feed has been filling up with photos and "love-yous" of fathers of my extended family and former students, but I'm not sure a picture does justice to the ways in which my father influenced me. If I could turn myself upside down and drain out the odds and ends with which my father filled my head, I'm not sure how much of just plain me there would be left. He and I didn't see eye to eye on many things, but I think we agreed on the *joys* of words and knowledge and literature and even teaching. (His past students, I have found, have their own store of D. Gow fun facts that he dropped on them in *his* four decades in the classroom.)

Love and support are wonderful things, and I guess in the end the ways these tended to manifest themselves in my relationship with my father, the compulsive teacher, is in what he taught me—the factoids and the attitudes and the ability to enjoy a painting.

I am also aware in my soul that from him I learned to see and accept students as both who they are and who they might be, and to be patient with each kid's process of becoming. He didn't much like my politics or my own progressive educational philosophy, but I am pretty sure he approved deep down of my vocation.

Not Your Father's School, June 15, 2014

WHY TEACH?

Perspective by Josie Holford, Head of School (retired), Poughkeepsie Day School

I first knew Peter through print. A prolific writer at NAIS and elsewhere he was an invaluable voice on all things educational. Then came the heady days of early social media—an open digital agora for the free exchange of ideas and ideals about schools and learning, innovation, and change. Finally educators could burst free of the confines of the classroom walls, find each other on line and build communities of learning. The sheen of that time has tarnished but the lasting impact of connection remains. Peter proved an excellent Twitter chat host and contributor. And his blog posts have provided an ongoing resource—a running commentary on the issues of the day and how to think about them. The "Not Your Father's School" series on strategic planning was memorable.

But then there was the real life Peter—the friend at NAIS, the good shepherd of ICG, and the natural collaborator who always showed up to lead, support, advise, and guide. Rereading these pieces I see how Peter has become one of those voices in my head: a guide on how to think about the business of school. At the heart of Peter's work is the belief that, by coming together around shared values, we can find the best ways forward. Teachers and teaching—the choices we make and how we go about the work—matter. It is wise voices like Peter's that help show us how to fuse good intentions with practical work in the service of what matters most: children and their growth as learners.

4 WHAT MAKES GREAT TEACHERS— AND WHAT ATTRACTS THEM TO SCHOOLS?

What seems like a long month ago a piece by Malcolm Gladwell appeared in the *New Yorker* under the title "Most Likely to Succeed." As is usual for Gladwell's work, the article is dazzlingly written, creatively constructed, and provocative; he loves being the gadfly. In this case, the conventional wisdom he is questioning has to do with teacher hiring, curiously mirrored against the process pro football uses to vet prospective recruits. The subtitle of the article is "How do we hire when we can't tell who's right for the job?" And that is his point.

I'm not going to offer up a critique of Gladwell's approach, although lately I've found his thinking on education to be surprisingly reactionary, but the article seems to have sparked yet another round of the "What's wrong with teachers?" discussion, this time among what is perhaps a more elevated crowd than that stirred up by campaigning politicians. I was interested to note a few days later a blog post on the *Wall Street Journal* "The Juggle" site entitled "What Makes a Good Teacher?" The post made reference to the Gladwell piece and was clearly inspired by it. Interested, I followed the commentary on this post, which revealed to me a great deal about how the kinds of Americans who read the *Journal* and the *New Yorker* think about teachers and schools.

Predictably, a fair number of the *Journal* commentarists let loose on teacher unions, tenure, and contemporary approaches to the teaching of spelling and grammar—the usual shibboleths of conservative educational critics. There was a biting and thus entertaining exchange over the proper use of the apostrophe, as in "it's" versus "its," and a couple of writers just thought the U.S. should adopt whatever methods are used to teach math and science in countries whose students outscore their American peers on the TIMMS assessment. A few people sneered at what they assume to be the poor intellectual quality of those who enter teacher training programs. One respondent even dragged out his (alleged?) SAT score as proof of his own intellectual worth.

But there was also a great deal of thoughtful commentary on the nature of schools and the qualities of excellent teachers and the kinds of conditions under which teachers can thrive. It was heartening in the end to see how many of the writers (and a few of them are teachers, I'll have to admit) seem to understand the challenges of teaching.

Stepping way back, I will go so far as to generalize that a deep concern for children and their success was, by consensus, the signal characteristic of good teachers. Those who have this quality are seen as willing to make some sacrifices, even Herculean efforts, to make sure their students learn and grow.

Excellent teaching happens, the writers tended to agree, where teachers have the time to prepare adequately and the administrative support to be innovative in their pedagogy. A few even acknowledged that *Journal* readers are likely to live in communities where affluence and high expectations around education are pretty much a guarantee of satisfactory educational outcomes; one writer even pointed out that socioeconomic filters tend to blunt the effects of the problems with teacher hiring that Gladwell writes about.

None of the *Journal* commenters nor Gladwell himself explicitly mentioned what I believe to be another factor in teacher success: clarity of purpose. (I even dashed off a letter to the editor of the *New Yorker*, but I'm not expecting it to appear. [And it didn't.])

Schools with strong, clear and easily understood missions and the will to put these missions at the center of everything they do—generally independent schools, most religious private schools, and many charter schools—are likely to attract teachers who will be willing to "go the extra mile" with students to enact and teach values and ideals in which they believe. Within this group, independent schools have both the historical and financial advantages to capture the attention of prospective teachers with especially strong qualifications, to evaluate candidates carefully and fully (and expensively), and to offer contracts that, even if salaries are less than those of some charter schools, do not generally equate to vows of poverty.

Not every independent school teacher is a great teacher or even a good one, but schools that are exceptionally clear about who they need as teachers and who can communicate their educational and cultural values well in the hiring process are likely to attract and retain particularly strong faculties. Independent schools have another advantage here, in that longevity and established governance structures add a layer of mission and program stability that is not to be found in every charter school or newly founded faith-based school.

What Malcolm Gladwell may not have considered, and what the *Journal* writers seem to have missed, is that the kinds of teachers who will establish the success-oriented relationships with their students and who will spend hours perfecting their curriculum and pedagogy are most likely to be found in schools that educate their students and nurture their teachers in a context of shared meaning and purpose, supported from every quarter in the school and its community. (One wonders whether the TIMMS poster-child countries are those in which cultural homogeneity and a longstanding sense of teachers as figures of respect create this context on a national level, at least within the education system.)

It would be a wonderful world if our politicians would create more conditions for public schools in which meaning, purpose, and reward structures commensurate with the importance of the enterprise were the rule and not the exception. Places where any teacher can find meaning and purpose would attract the great candidates every school and every student deserves.

In the meantime, private schools, and in particular independent schools, should continue to work hard to enunciate and live positive, distinctive missions and values. This should ensure a continual flow of great, and potentially great, teachers toward their classrooms.

Admirable Faculties, January 8, 2009

5 RESTITUTIONAL TEACHING: A THOUGHT ON WHY WE (OR AT LEAST SOME OF US MAY) TEACH

I have had some wonderful teachers in my life—a solid bunch in my public elementary school and another group in my independent junior high–high school. They shaped and influenced my life in ways I wish I could still tell them about; I've managed to get to the survivors, but all of this was long ago.

But I've had some serious clinkers, too: a trio of junior high and high school math teachers who killed off what had been a real enthusiasm, and too many senior teachers and a school head in high school who contrived to create an overall ethos so redolent of "guilty until proven innocent" that even my goody-goody self was often uncomfortable and unhappy.

I confess I've also come to resent that my all-boys independent secondary school offered essentially nothing by way of instruction in the arts, presumably because such pursuits were neither suitably manly nor "rigorously academic" in the way the Old Guard there defined the term. I had loved my regular and well taught art and music classes in elementary school and had been encouraged by the teachers to further pursue both.

Which brings me to an observation I've been making for years but never fully explored: that there is something that I call "restitutional teaching," the idea that for some of us a portion of our motivation is to see to it that what was done unto us or our friends as children is not done unto others: the squashing of spirit and passion, the dehydration of subject matter until it was truly arid and meaningless, the petty and often unintentional unfairnesses and humiliations that can scar kids for a lifetime.

In any event, it's not so much of a surprise that I've spent the last 35 years, after a bit of casting around, in a progressive-founded coed school with multiple thriving and excellent arts programs and an aggressively student-centered culture. It's perhaps even less of a surprise that my boss, our head, is a graduate of the same high school I attended, where he was perhaps less of a goody-goody (he'll own that, I think) and must have been uncomfortable even more often than I was. We've never discussed this, incidentally, but here we are, working to make sure that our kids aren't squashed and mistrusted and that the pedagogy and curriculum are engaging and even—shock!—often quite fun.

(I should also add with emphasis here that our alma mater has transformed itself into a place where the arts are huge and kids seem to have a great deal of fun while still working, playing, and creating hard. I would happily work or send my own kids there now.)

And over the years I've run into way more than a handful of teachers at all levels who acknowledge a restitutional motivation behind their work and choice of schools. Little red dots appear magically under "restitutional" as I type to indicate that it's not a real word, but it Googles up quite nicely with citations in the context of restorative justice, which I quite like. A fair number of us, I think, have stayed the course because the last few decades have tended to honor ideas like student-centeredness, creativity, and justice as a concept both at large and in classrooms and administrative offices. A few years ago I wrote a [book called *The Intentional Teacher*](), and I suppose that few things are more intentional than the idea of staying in the biz to enact the Golden Rule in the special sense of teaching others as you *would wish to have been* taught, instead of as you *were* taught.

There are other, similar motivations, and in time I'll try to address some of these. A chill is passing through me at the moment as I wonder whether there are other educators, perhaps more deeply scarred than "restitutionals," who practice "retributive teaching," à la Hogwarts's Severus Snape or Dolores Umbridge (what must have happened to *her* as a schoolgirl?). I shall try to let this idea disapparate.

I should stress, incidentally, that I didn't seethe my way through college and graduate school with a clearly defined restitutional intent. Rather, the notion took form somewhere in my first couple of years at Beaver Country Day School, where I realized that I was somehow "home" in ways that I hadn't felt at other schools and then began to ponder why that might be. In time the idea coalesced into a pole toward which my personal lodestone could point, and there I was. Maybe I give myself too much credit for intentionality; perhaps it was just a shoe that fit when I wore it.

So if you are among the teachers who occasionally reference the idea that we've gotta give kids better experiences than those that we had in school, welcome to the world of restitutional teaching. Perhaps the real intentionality in all this is the understanding that in order to do our best for kids we need to keep thinking and learning about every aspect of our work. Even if restoring karmic balance in our personal educational universe is a fundamental reflex, we can't just do it on autopilot.

Not Your Father's School, July 16, 2014

6 PAYING IT FORWARD: FURTHER THOUGHTS ON WHY WE (OR AT LEAST SOME OF US MAY) TEACH

In my last post I suggested that a powerful motivation for some teachers seems to have been a desire to "correct" the teaching that they themselves experienced. I probably implied, without meaning to, that this is a sole impetus for those "restitutional" teachers, as if they were only driven by a desire to fix the teaching thing, at least for their own students.

I realize that this isn't quite fair, and, like most human endeavor, the motivations for most of us are complicated and manifold.

As much, for example, as I have been pleased to work for many years in an environment that seems to offer an antidote to some of my own experiences, I am also aware of and grateful to the many fine teachers that I had and whose efforts, and occasionally whose style, I have hoped to emulate, in some way to continue or carry forward the gift that they gave me. If restitution is a powerful motivator, so is what might be called paying it forward. There are moments when I realize that my career has been a poor tribute to many of those who taught me.

In my public elementary school this includes some of my homeroom teachers (I've [written elsewhere](#) that, c. 1956, Southside Elementary School in East Aurora, New York, looped first and second grades; Miss Garrett was my lucky draw for those years) and especially the art teacher, Mrs. Jost, who encouraged me to follow my interest as far as I could. Mrs. Larrison thought I could sing and hoped I might pick up the violin, although history will have disappointed her in both respects. Miss Brock was a rookie third-grade teacher who saw me through a very tough personal year by simply being who she was. The veteran Mrs. Boldt was the platonic ideal of a fifth-grade teacher; she treated us all with enormous respect and taught with equally enormous compassion and the common sense born of her other life as a dairy farm wife, up with the cows long before school opened and responsible for charges far more needy even than a bunch of ten year-olds. "Arithmetic" classes in grades five and six were homogeneous, and Miss Reali taught us such marvels as Zeno's Paradox and lattice multiplication to get my fifth-grade group excited about math. (In writing this I discover that I also remember the first names of most of these teachers, but in respect I name them here as I called them back in the Eisenhower era.)

Junior high, off in the independent day school in the nearby city, wasn't that different, although a couple of serious clinkers inspired the more restitutional aspects of my future work. But Mr. Ohler, who later proved to be a veritable Socrates when it came to encouraging slightly older teenagers to think for themselves, badgered me in seventh grade to read the sports and comic pages and be a bit more human, or at least well rounded, in my outlook on popular culture. Mr. Herlan—still a Facebook friend, by gosh!—taught that iron discipline could sustain a certain amount of ironic humor. Mr. Gurney's foray into teaching from the law may have had mixed results for him, but the debates and mock trials we created in that class, chaotic as it may have looked to him and his supervisors, was one of the great learning experiences of my life. Mr. Hayes gave the enduring gift of Latin, which I am teaching these days in small doses, and the equally enduring memory of a tall and serious man in dignified middle age leading locomotive cheers of "Let's get a hundred!" at exam time.

High school had its share of both greats and highly capable eccentrics, and kids probably ought to experience a few of each. Mr. Sutter taught Spanish trying to channel Severus Snape but too easily revealed his sense of humor and affection for his students. Mr. Sessions lectured, kind of, while leaning perilously far back in a castered, sprung wooden office chair, raining brilliance on us as we tracked the frequency with which he used some of his pet phrases. We failed to appreciate at the time that teaching modern East Asian history in 1966 was a bold and even radical step; we would otherwise probably have been memorizing the succession of English monarchs or the like. And at last, as a junior and then blessedly again as a senior, I had Mr. Strachan, the math teacher who explained things well, had patience with my deficits, and might possibly, with a bit more time, have turned me into an actual mathematician.

I had great professors in college, notably the enigmatic Harold Bloom (he of extreme and often controversial positions), who taught American poetry (his first class on the topic) with his face buried in his hands and had all the ambitious graduate students in the class hanging on his every word. Three generous and concerned professors took pains to eviscerate the self-conscious writing style I had learned in high school, last of all Mr. Loewenberg, a graduate student whose wise and scathing comments on my final paper of senior year presaged the misery that would be graduate school for me. Mr. Westphal, Mr. Kasson, and above all my advisor for two senior theses, the amazing Norman Holmes Pearson, demonstrated that college professors are human beings, too. My freshman History and Politics professor was a student of Leo Strauss named W. M. Kendrick—a complete enigma then (our classes were sometimes held in a secure undisclosed location) and still to this day; I managed not to become a Straussian convert like so many of the Neocons (hey, including Dick Cheney, speaking of secure undisclosed locations) who brought us the Iraq War.

I chose my path to graduate school unwisely, but my spouse has reminded me that everywhere you've been is on the road to where you are. It was Mr. Boulger who finally helped me devise an appropriate exit strategy as well as helping me at last to appreciate English Romantic poetry.

As the title of this blog hints and many posts have confirmed, a huge influence on my teaching life, if not my actual style, was my late father, David Gow. My uncle, Norman W. Howard, was also a role model. I have limited myself in this enumeration to people actually called teachers by trade, but I have learned much from too many others to even start mentioning here.

Yes, I am enjoying naming names, and the chances are I am forgetting some others who are worthy of mention here. The point is, of course, that most of us who teach, I think, could proclaim their own roll call of great and influential teachers in their lives, and in our daily work I like to think we are all paying tribute to those men and women whose influence we may have recognized too late, or perhaps too fleetingly, to express our gratitude in a timely way.

Naming these names here is also my feeble and much belated way of saying thank you. I rather hope I've done a better job simply by working in their spirit.

Not Your Father's School, July 20, 2014

EDUCATION, FROM THE OUTSIDE LOOKING IN

Perspective by Debi Ellman, *Associate Director of College Counseling, Beaver Country Day School*

In this collection of posts, Peter, esteemed teacher, administrator, consultant, and most gratefully, my forty-year mentor and friend, reflects upon our current educational climate through a stereoscopic lens. In a reflective, personal, and engaging voice, he intertwines the past and present, dispelling educational myths and exposing cracks in our current educational landscape. In "Your Father's (and Grandparents') Teachers: A Measured Appreciation," Peter imagines the teachers of his grandfather's day wheeling in chairs of contemporary classrooms, and (despite contrary notions) feeling, fundamentally, at home. In "People of My Village," Peter offers a glimpse of his childhood neighborhood, a rural village like so many still dotting our states, that is rich in relationships and values but lacking in resources. He presents, in his blog post, a persuasive plea for addressing the needs of rural public schools across America. In "The Original Disruptor: A Cautionary reflection on *Dead Poets Society*," Peter casts a critical eye on the motives of "disruptive innovators," both past and present, who seek to satisfy their own personal needs over those of the students' whom they serve and stretch. Finally, In "Edu-porn," Peter illuminates the shortcomings of those who, promoting their own educational agendas, take delight in scathingly pointing out what's wrong with reform tactics of others rather than promoting change that genuinely meets students' needs. Reading Peter's posts will open your eyes to a broader frame for assessing educational reform. With a glance to our past, Peter speaks with passion and insight about pressing issues and concerns impacting education today.

7 YOUR FATHER'S (AND GRANDPARENTS') TEACHERS—A MEASURED APPRECIATION

I've preached hard on the need for schools to embrace change and innovation as they adapt their work to the requirements of a new age and new markets. The schools of tomorrow can't be like the schools of yesterday or even today, not in the way they think about curriculum and pedagogy; we can't be stuck in a rut.

I hope, though, I don't sound as though I despise everything that came before, uh, me, or that I'm one of those shrill voices condemning all the educational practices of the past as crimes against children—I'm not. This is my attempt to put some perspective on the relationship between "old times" and our own.

It's certainly conventional wisdom now to make the claim that schools today must produce something (that is to say, provide learning experiences for kids) substantially different from an old, "industrial" model. "Schools used to be in the knowledge distribution business," a friend has written, as if the essential measure of graduates in 1910 or 1950 had been in fact how much stuff—course content—they knew. (It makes me wonder a bit about the implied inverse, that we're no longer about either knowledge, or distribution, or both. But of course that's utterly wrong, too.)

I'm old enough, and I would maintain fortunate enough, to have spent time with grandparents who were all born in the nineteenth century, even before William McKinley became president—a long time ago. One was an educator, one a banker and civil servant, one a homemaker, and one an artist. All attended public schools in booming cities, two in the Midwest and two in the Northeast.

Except for the educator, who arguably spent a portion of his life passing along professionally some of what he had learned in his high school classes to his own students, I'm going to put forth the radical idea that what these worthy people took away from their pre-World War I high school experiences had no more to do with "knowledge," in the pejorative sense that we use it today as an agglomeration of facts and principles learned by rote, than what we want our students today to take away from their multimodal, multigenre collaborative problem-solving projects.

Somehow we have it in our heads that our forebears were treated like robots, trained in schools that beat into them knowledge, like the ability to diagram sentences and decline Latin nouns, that was regarded as necessary preparation for work on the factory floor, a pre-marriage career in the stenography pool, or the life of a traveling salesman. Teachers of this era, we surmise, were apparently equally robotic, fortified (intoxicated, even) by their ability to inflict corporal punishment and no more understanding of the ways their students thought or learned than they were of Professor Einstein's latest equations. In this formulation, the poorly trained teachers in the old, "industrial" model depended on brute force to disseminate pointless knowledge, because that is what the Industrial Age demanded of its workers and their families.

Arrant and even arrogant nonsense! say I. Whoever was teaching my grandmothers and grandfathers (or yours, I dare say), probably had no more belief that the facts their students were asked to learn (all those dates—the worst!) were required for a meaningful life than you do when you ask students to learn the essential content that underlies the big concepts on which those projects are based. If the teachers of yore didn't know basic neuroscience or Piagetian theories of development, the best of them learned from their students (as most of us still do, day in and day out) what they really needed to know (as human teachers, not robots): how their students thought, how they acquired understanding, what motivated them, and what turned them off.

It may have been a bit less elegant than our more scientific ways, but in the hands and hearts of patient, caring people, it was "knowledge" enough to inspire millions of children and to help shape their characters in particular directions. If wrists were slapped or humiliations inflicted, such were the unfortunate vagaries of the times as well as the probably uneven quality and nature of teachers and their lives—and there are still plenty of educators, even in these enlightened times, who have been known to "blow it" and do something stupid and cruel and dismissive; you can slam the door on a child's aspirations just as easily via Smartboard or email as from the chalky dais of an airless Victorian classroom. We still have our share of "bad"—or at least vocationally misdirected—teachers, even with all we know about psychology and the art of hiring.

Nor did the portraits of Washington and Lincoln on their classroom walls make my grandparents into mindless jingoists, any more than knowing a smidgen of Latin made them into successful workers or parents. What the grandparents took away from school was not rote knowledge, but an understanding of how they learned, the idea that there would always be more to learn, and in some sense how the world outside their own households functioned. In their later lives they diverged (as people do) into Republicans and Democrats, smokers and disapprovers, family-driven and civically engaged, workaholics and dreamers, voters (in time) and scoffers. The skills they learned in school were not any more or less appropriate to their dramatically changing times (Think about my maternal grandmother: born 1896, died compos mentis 1992—what must it have been like to live through that span?) as the vaunted "21st-century skills" we ask our students to learn today.

I have to believe, even if public discourse in their day didn't make much of these ideas, that the best of the men and women who taught my grandparents held in their teacher minds the notion that intellectual curiosity and flexibility, a kind of suppleness of thought and the ability and disposition to keep on learning, were central to what they were trying to get across in the classroom. We ought not dismiss their motives, even if it is easy for us to pooh-pooh the model that memorizing Latin parts of speech or German verbs was good training for learning how to use, say, an electric vacuum cleaner or adapt to the evolution of automobile pedal function and placement from the Model T to the 1958 Oldsmobile.

I will happily grant that the kind of "real world" problem-solving and a number of modern practices in curriculum and assessment design probably move us and our schools closer to helping students connect school learning to the development of lifelong curiosity and adaptability than did exhaustive grammar exercises or memorizing lists of English monarchs. But I am not going to condemn the teachers of the past as pedantic or unenlightened automata nor the schools in which they taught as nothing more than brutalizing assembly lines of thoughtless, heartless learning. Even a cursory look at the experiences of real people (because I cannot believe that my small family sample is unique) indicates that they merit far better.

I imagine a magical circumstance in which the teachers who encouraged my grandfather (the teacher) to apply to college and who prevailed on his millworker parents to give their son a shot at higher education were suddenly transported, in a sort of reverse Connecticut Yankee way, to a classroom at my own school in 2011. They might have to update their chops as teachers (and they might actually be extremely relieved at being liberated from drilling students on material they themselves might have found dull), but I think their instincts and hopes for their students would put them right in the best kind of groove as effective educators in our time. They clearly believed in kids and put their most effective time and energy not into diagramming sentences but into helping kids reach worthwhile goals in ways that would enrich their whole lives.

Not Your Father's School, September 13, 2011

8 THE PEOPLE OF MY VILLAGE

It happened again the other day, when I started a story, "In my village...."

Apparently, this is hysterically funny. Villages, it seems, don't happen any more in the kind of world where someone like me could possibly live, and in living memory they never have. Over-educated, middle-class, straight, cisgender white Americans of Boomer age cannot have come from villages. Suburbs, yes, small towns, yes, cities—of course! But not villages. Villages are, like, in Central America or someplace where students go on community service trips.

But I come from a village—we often called it a hamlet, even. A few hundred people lived there when I was a kid in the Eisenhower years; there might even be a thousand now, as some of the people fleeing the nearby city during its dramatic economic collapse in the 1970s bought and built on some of the view-ciferous ridgelines out Center Street or up on Vermont Hill. The village center when I was growing up consisted of a building that contained a one-chair barber shop, the post office, and a Frontier filling station. Across the street was a tavern (euphemized as a "hotel") that also served food and had a couple of bowling lanes. Catty-corner from this was a Red & White grocery store that sold basics including kerosene and cookies by the unit, as in "May I have two Fig Newtons, please, Missus Cornell?" The library came to the village every other week in form of the county Bookmobile truck that parked by the disused two-room schoolhouse and managed to smell just like a small-town library should—of books and paste and a bit of mildew!

In my village there was a stoplight on the state highway, and the speed limit was 40 for a half mile or so on either side of the stoplight. Up the road there was an Atlantic station where my family bought our leaded gasoline. Down the side street that met Route 16 at the stoplight were a row of houses civilized by a few hundred yards of disintegrating concrete sidewalk, a Presbyterian church, and the old schoolhouse that had been converted a town court by 1960. There was the tiny cluster of frame buildings—dormitories, the Main Building, the Lab, and the Shop—that comprised the campus of the school my grandfather had started and where my father taught.

Besides the teachers at the school and the three or four kitchen and building and grounds workers, there were plenty of people who worked in the village. No, not at the businesses by the stoplight, which employed maybe half a dozen people in total, but on their own farms, mostly dairy. Villagers did their real shopping, banking, and doctoring in one of the towns, each five miles away, on the state road. The northern town was larger, maybe 5,000 people in the mid Fifties, with two banks and two supermarkets and even some clothing stores; it was only about 25 miles from the city and a couple of newer neighborhoods had even become a bit suburban after World War II. The southern one was smaller; its big businesses were a candle factory, a wholesale florist (with gift shop!), and a Ford dealer who sold both cars and tractors. We did most of our business in the town to the north—which in New York State practice is still officially a "village," too, at least the part that is most densely populated.

I belabor this point because people need way too many reminders in 2015 that there are still millions of Americans who live in villages like mine—call them villages or hamlets or just wide spots in the road with a convenience store and maybe a 40 zone. Poverty lives in these villages, too, not just on the main roads, but in the hills and valleys nearby. The internet is available in many of these places only at a high cost, compounding socioeconomic want with cultural isolation.

The people of my village are not funny, and they're not irrelevant, although our urbanized, tech-ed up, hipster world tends to think of them as characters from some bygone sitcom. The people of my village are Americans who are trying to figure it all out, trying to achieve the dream even as they watch the money all go somewhere else and where all they see on television are cities and suburbs, some suffering and some wealthy, but all reminding them that as country folk they are out of it.

And the people of my village want a good education for their children and wonder why the money and the attention and the cheap internet service all seem to go to cities with epically (per the local news reports) underperforming schools or to the wealthy suburban districts whose team uniforms always look brand new. Small public schools, rural public schools, still exist, and they want to thrive, just as their teachers and students want to thrive in a culture that barely acknowledges their existence.

This blog may be an odd place to make a plea for rural public schools and to be reminding readers that poverty and lack of opportunity in rural America are just as corrosive and destructive as they are in our cities. I admit that I drank the cultural Kool-Aid and melted into the metro Northeastern sprawl long ago, but I think of my village often, and I don't think of it as a joke line. It's the Christmas season, and when I go home, I go to my village.

Not Your Father's School, December 23, 2015

9 THE ORIGINAL DISRUPTOR: A CAUTIONARY REFLECTION ON *DEAD POETS SOCIETY*

The tragic death of Robin Williams has moved us all, no matter what our special memories of his oeuvre might be: Mork, Adrian Cronauer, Peter Pan, or even John Jacob Jingleheimer Schmidt in one of my favorite films, *To Wong Foo Thanks for Everything, Julie Newmar*.

For many teachers, of course, Williams's iconic role was the iconoclastic Mr. Keating in *Dead Poets Society*. Here is the teacher many of us Baby Boomers wanted to be, a no-bullshit smart-ass who cut to the chase in his dealings with students, parents, and administrators and who seemed to prevail (until vocational martyrdom) in the face of hidebound tradition and the disapproval of his peers. Who among us has not stood upon at least a chair, if not a desk, at some early point in our careers, calling down the fire and brimstone of Truth upon the platitudes and perceived acquiescence of the past, trying to bring our students to enlightenment with shock and awe?

I find myself wondering whether the fascination of many educators (including yours truly) with "disruptive innovation" wasn't first inspired by Williams's bravura performance. Even the film's title tweaks the nose of the canon of "dead white males" that we eagerly pushed aside to make way for new voices representing previously suppressed experiences and perspectives.

I suspect that every teacher, deep down, wants to represent the future, wants to be the teacher who gets through to their students as no one has before, who brings them to that enlightenment. Those of us who have brought new and occasionally unusual methods into our practice—even methods from handed down from the halls of academe (places like Project Zero, its very name forged on the anvil of disruptive innovation: "starting from zero")—have felt ourselves to be iconoclasts, and all too often administrators, colleagues, parents, and sometimes even students have happily played the role of resisting traditionalists, fueling our narrative of heroic (or at least admirably necessary) disruption. And if Williams as John Keating wasn't our sole inspiration, we can look to earlier models like Glenn Ford's character in *The Blackboard Jungle* and Sidney Poitier's in *To Sir, With Love*. We learned early that effective teaching requires special insights and a willingness to push students out of their comfort zones.

The question is whether moving students out of their comfort zones is sometimes just a way of pulling them into ours. As any elementary or middle school teacher knows, disruptors can also be displaying a need for attention, and most of us are aware that too much charisma, too much clever poking at student complacency, can sometimes be a dangerous quality in a teacher, disruption feeding personal need that sometimes crosses boundaries not of tradition but of personal trust.

My father, for the record, found *Dead Poets Society* profoundly disturbing, not because of Mr. Keating's courageous stand against apathy but because in Keating's methods, in his obvious needs, my father saw danger. Keating transformed his many of his students' perspectives, yes, but the price was high, paid in a student's life, a fact we have tended to forget as we celebrate the extraordinary scenes like "food for worms" and "O Captain". My father refused to see Keating as a hero, nor even an antihero.

But as we continue our love affair with disruptive innovation, it's worth taking a moment to reflect on what lies behind some of our own urges to make change happen, to upset the apple cart. We believe we are right, believe we are onto something important, and from Noah to Jesus in the Temple to John Keating we have worthy models of what it means to march proudly and loudly to the beat of one's own drummer in the face of implacable opposition.

Sometimes, though, there's an element of melodrama to the narrative we create as we push new, unfamiliar, and sometimes unpopular educational ideas forward, and we have to remember that we are not and cannot be the stars of some kind of "disruption theater." To push a metaphor, we may fancy ourselves to be the captains of the educational ship, may secretly even want to be "my captain" to our students, but they are neither the passengers nor the cargo but in fact the shipowners and navigators. Our job is to serve students' needs and to let these needs be master of our fates, not the other way around.

Not Your Father's School, August 12, 2014

10   EDU-PORN

A smart blogger at *Toxic Culture* lately identified as "edu-porn" those feel-good articles and films that show a well-meaning rebel thinking outside the box and transforming schools and classrooms, one caring little environment at a time. Ever since Mr. Daddy-O decided to come back for another round of teaching would-be juvenile delinquents in the 1956 film *Blackboard Jungle*, audiences and voters have been comforted to know that one person can make a difference in schools, at least until they leave (as Evan Hunter, author of *The Blackboard Jungle*, the novel on which the film was based, did after 17 days as a teacher).

But there is another kind of edu-porn, the sadomasochist side of the genre, that gets an awful lot of airplay these days and that must offer the same frisson of pleasure to its purveyors that those teacher-savior stories provide.

I am talking about the mountains of statistics—seldom represented by the same numbers twice, so it seems—that "prove" that American children are falling ever farther behind their peers in other nations, particularly those with growing economies in Asia. These numbers are regularly hauled out by commentators on the right and increasingly the left as evidence that our schools are failing, our children are doomed, and our society and our nation are plummeting into irrelevancy.

I don't even care whether these numbers, based on all kinds of comparative test data, are right or wrong; in the aggregate I know that they are real and alarming. What concerns me is that I have long sensed a kind of weird, cruel "I-told-you-so" pleasure among some of those who are most eager to tell us that the children of China, India, Singapore, Japan, and Finland are soon going to be our superiors in the global economic and political order; better start learning Mandarin so that we'll have a few interlocutors who will be able to speak with our new overseers!

Often enough the blame for this trend, which goes back to the post-Sputnik era in its most statistical and malevolent form, seems directed at whatever version of "progressive education" the blamer has created in his or her own mind and doesn't like.

Mathematics instruction—which is clearly in need of improvement in the U.S., with Singapore and Japanese models offering promise—usually tops the list of curricular and pedagogical culprits, but "multiculturalism," project-based instruction, school schedules and calendars, and of course anything associated with the word "self-esteem" are among the usual suspects. I think that I occasionally catch a whiff of regret among the most vitriolic of education critics that the American education system has invited girls, and then students of color, into the classrooms where white boys once reigned, and of course there is the strange and paradoxically countervailing abhorrence of "elites" and elitism that lets the harshest critics have it both ways: hating both the education system and those who have succeeded within it.

Clearly those who have expressed hope that the Obama presidency will fail—regardless of all the human suffering that would accompany the kind of failure for which they most hope—are a model for a kind of political *schadenfreude* that is equally turned on by the idea that American schools are failing and that American children are victims of this failure. This stance lets those who are just plain cynical claim at least equal airtime with those who propose legitimate or at least well-meaning solutions, from charter schools to vouchers to serious reform. In the avalanche of dreadful numbers, it's hard to see who is offering real hope and who are just gratified by watching educators and the initiatives of the past three or five or twenty decades twist in the wind.

Of late I have noted from the more progressive side of the field some of the same. In particular, some of the strongest (and in some cases most on-point) advocates around technology in education and "21st-century skills" can sometimes be heard pronouncing the same kind of doom on education and educators, suggesting that the "failure" to move forward quickly enough toward a more tech-informed, more New Progressive approach to teaching and learning is a kind of crime being practiced on children. Like angry educational conservatives who believe they know it all and take pleasure in pointing out the failings of education as it is currently practiced, the more shrill voices on the other end of the spectrum risk turning their critiques into the kind of splenetic, empty rhetoric that makes them feel good and impedes real progress.

Sadomasochistic edu-porn is not, apparently, the province of the right only, but I hope that those who are most sincere and thoughtful in their efforts to reform the system can restrain their delight in pointing out what's wrong and focus rather on moving the American educational system toward what is effective and what best meets the real needs of all children.

The New Progressive, February 3, 2010

FINDING THE TEACHERS WE NEED

Perspective by Greg Martin, *Upper School Dean,*
Perkiomen School

It always amazing me the reaction I get from people when I tell them I am a teacher at a boarding school. Confusion, questions about students, assumptions as to what a boarding school is, etc. Outside of the normal conversations surrounding public education, few people seem to recognize the independent school industry as a whole, notwithstanding the myths and assumptions carried about these types of schools. As well, there seems to be little thought as to the people who teach in independent school classrooms: who they are, why they do it, what their backgrounds and competencies are, and what views on education they hold. With nearly three-quarters of a million students being educated in independent schools by roughly seventy-five thousand teachers, the independent school world is far larger than many think, nearly equaling the number of students and teachers found in the entire state of Massachusetts. Teachers are the engines that drive schools. They deliver programs, populate buildings, and create the relationships that define independent school education. They are multi-talented and often wear many hats. As well, they are not recognized in the world of "education" due to the fact that many don't hold state credentials and haven't gone through traditional teacher preparation programs. Yet somehow, they succeed. The independent school educator thrives on independence, away from state guidelines, standardized tests, canned curricula, and detached school boards.

I met Peter Gow while doing research for my dissertation. A "big name" in the independent school world, Peter was approachable from the start. Happy to engage in conversation and always up for a go at the tough questions independent schools are facing. A "teacher's teacher," Peter has lived the life of the "triple threat" educator at a boarding school, been a classroom teacher, administrator, consultant, advisor, and mentor. In every capacity, Peter understands that the independent school educator is a unique combination of intellect, emotional intelligence, artistic and/or athletic skill, pastoral care, and rebel. Over the years, Peter researched and wrote and good deal about the independent schoolteacher and while the roles continue to evolve and shift, Peter continues to hit the nail on the head in viewing the independent school educator as a special type of person. The circumstances and surroundings of the independent school world necessitate a multi-talented team of teachers to deliver a value-added program to a diverse group of students. In doing so, these educators prove they are deserving of some time in the spotlight; receiving attention and accolades for the fine work they do. Who better than Peter to write on the topic, as it truly takes one to know one?

11 HAS YOUR SCHOOL DONE ITS "HIRING SELF-STUDY" YET?

The hiring season is about to begin, and there is no better time than the first weeks after the holiday break is over for schools to undertake what I call the "hiring self-study." This is a chance for the principal actors in the school's hiring process to sit down and do a bit of big-picture pre-reflection on the season to come.

Rather than concentrating on the individual positions to be filled, the hiring self-study should address "essential questions," such as "What kinds of teachers have succeeded here?" and "What are some of the needs of the school community that the hiring season gives us an opportunity to address?" If the school has undertaken exit interviews with departing faculty in the past few years, this is a great time to pull out the data from these and ponder aspects of school culture that have come up in those interviews. (It is to be hoped that this data has been looked at previously, in the broader context of examining school culture.) It's a great time to do some "blue sky" imagining around possibilities that are congruent with strategic aims but not necessarily on the immediate radar—global studies or green initiatives, perhaps, or ramping up a service program. Like curriculum work, hiring is very much about mission and values, and now is the time to consider who these might play out or be furthered by the cohort of new teachers.

It's almost always a good idea to include issues of diversity in this process; the best time to make an internal commitment to certain goals in the process is before the actual recruiting begins. The "self-study" might also include a thoughtful critique of past recruiting campaigns and some brainstorming on better approaches.

It might not be a bad time to review the materials the school uses to recruit, from its "employment at" webpages to the boilerplate text that accompanies print ads to any kind of printed material that relates to working at the school. The idea is to give prospective candidates as accurate and positive a picture as possible of what it is like to be a member of the school community. Perhaps the school could invite its contacts at teacher placement agencies to come to the campus for a sit-down and a tour, as agency workers with a good knowledge of the school can give candidates the most thoughtful and focused guidance as well as understanding key factors in a making a great match.

Similarly, this is the time to determine how the school will handle internal candidacies—timing of postings, whether or not to offer "courtesy interviews," or how to handle any tricky political issues that can be anticipated.

The last thing that should be included in the hiring self-study is a review of the internal process by which candidates will be contacted and brought in for interviews. How will the paperwork flow, who will be making initial contacts, who will be involved in interviews, and what conditions must be met before an offer can be made? I'm a big fan of centralizing the starting point of the process with a single contact person to whom resumes will be sent from agencies or random applicants and who will be the nominal addressee for inquiries based on advertisements or postings; this reduces the chance that good candidates will be lost in the shuffle or otherwise overlooked.

A couple of years back I presented on "Managing the Hiring Process" at an NAIS Annual Conference. Here is the slideshow from that presentation, which covers the whole process from hiring self-study through induction: Recruiting and Hiring Independent School Teachers

Admirable Faculties, December 27, 2009

12 "EMPLOYMENT AT" SCHOOL WEBPAGES

I'm writing this from Canada, where I will be speaking at the Canadian Association of Independent Schools conference for school heads on the subject of "Building Faculties." It's hard not to have been distracted by financial turmoil as I have been putting my presentation together, with grim scenarios of hiring and salary freezes or worse spinning through my head. It's pretty certain that we'll see some enrollment reductions, and schools are already figuring out how to tighten their belts. "Holding Faculties Together in Tough Times" may be next year's topic.

Maybe, in the worst cases, either hiring new teachers won't be necessary, or maybe there will be so many people in the job market looking for anything that every open teaching job will attract hordes of qualified applicants. But I don't really think things will necessarily reach that point.

Experience tells me, and I'll admit that others may have data to contradict me, that tough times may actually mean that excellent teachers become harder to find. This may be because veterans elect to stay where they are or because independent school teaching looks like an economically vulnerable luxury service to young people looking to start careers. What this experience suggests to me, however, is that in a recession schools may find themselves in the ironic position of having to look even harder for teachers.

One point I'm going to make to my audience in Canada is that individual schools' "employment at" (or "jobs at" or "careers at") webpages are in need of some sprucing up. No longer is it enough just to list job openings, formal descriptions, and contact information. Hiring webpages need to be thoughtful, appealing, and as specific and informative as possible not just about today's job postings but also about what it is like to work at the school.

College admission websites are pretty good models here; for a number of years now the Massachusetts Institute of Technology, for example, has used student and admission-office bloggers to give something of the flavor of day to day life at M.I.T., and prospective students can find out anything they want by contacting someone in the admission office at any university. While this level of response to the merely interested may not be feasible for schools' hiring sites, the up-close-and-personal aspect of blogs written by a couple of teachers and perhaps even students seems like a great way to give candidates a sense of what it means to belong to a school community.

If the school already has blogs, virtual tours, or other interactive and "insider view" materials on its admission or other webpages, the hiring pages need to link directly to these. The same goes for online newspapers or literary magazines, sports pages, and anything else that reveals the school as it is. If the school has some great materials or information to share about teaching in particular, make these easily available for the world to see.

It's also never a bad idea to offer what one can regarding the community and region in which the school is situated. Cultural opportunities, outdoor resources, or other aspects of life that might attract teaching candidates should be a part of the "Work and Life at St. Basalt's" pages.

And even if prosperity turns out to be just around the corner as 2008 winds down, the challenge of attracting the very best teachers will remain. Schools often forget that prospective teachers make up a vital target audience for marketing materials, and, whether the future holds famine or feast, infusing the school's hiring webpages with real vitality seems like a great way to enhance the recruiting process for relatively little cost.

Admirable Faculties, October 17, 2008

13 RECRUITING STRATEGIES

In uncertain economic times the quality of a school's faculty matters more than ever, and the conditions of 2009 should occasion that smartest, most intentional hiring season ever. Whether the school is looking for one teacher or many, thoughtful recruiting—based on the hiring self-study recommended in a previous post as well as on the specific need—will increase the probability of bringing in appropriate candidates who, as teachers, will be able to deliver to students the programs on whose quality the school's reputation and well-being will depend.

Smart recruiting is mission-driven. The qualities of prospective teachers should match the stated and lived values and purposes of the school. Therefore, schools ought to think carefully about where they begin to post positions and cast their nets in search of candidates who will be good matches. No school should rely exclusively on agencies and hiring fairs to meet their needs, although these can be great sources of outstanding candidates; neither should schools automatically table applications that come in "out of the blue." Agencies, incidentally, are more than willing to work very closely with schools to match candidates, and whoever is in charge of a school's hiring should not be afraid to push agency contacts in search of the right people.

In recent years most independent schools have expressed a desire to make diversity an important part of their recruiting efforts, but frequently the challenges of a what is too often described as a "small pool" give schools an excuse to abandon this goal; working harder at this is the answer. This is an unfortunate situation that at its worst can breed some cynicism in the school community among those committed to diversity, but any school can make the extra effort needed to expand the reach of its recruiting efforts. At the very least, organizations like StrateGenius and NEMNET, which both offer underrepresented minority placement services, should be consulted at the outset of the hiring season.

To begin with, schools should explore local recruiting resources. Job listings for teaching positions can be posted in local newspapers, and such listings increasingly show up on sites such as Craig's List—it's not crazy to recruit where more and more people actually go looking. If there are local or regional publications where an inexpensive small display ad about "working at St. Basalt's" would attract attention, consider using such an ad as a conduit for contact with the school; this will be most cost-effective in cases where the school is making multiple hires.

In communities or regions with newspapers or on-line publications focused on traditionally underserved populations, want-ads for teaching jobs—even translated into languages other than English, if appropriate—are likely to reach potential candidates who might not be "hooked into" the agency or job fair scene or who might not know about school "jobs" webpages or regional association listing sites. Additionally, such ads are signals to a community that the school is thoughtful about its desire to participate in a multicultural world and sincere in its desire to have a diverse faculty, and such messages can attract new student applicants, as well. (In fact, all teacher-recruiting materials should be considered as having a role in student recruitment, and vice-versa.)

The content of the school's position listings is important. Some ads make schools sound so august and formal as to be potentially off-putting, while others supply so little information about either the position or the school as to be practically useless. Boilerplate language about the school should be concise but as warm as possible, and job descriptions should leave enough room for flexibility so that qualified candidates who do not fit a precise description are not discouraged. Visual content should be inviting; it is possible that the school seal and Latin motto are better left out or replaced simply by the school name in its official font.

I have written elsewhere on "employment at" websites, which should be made as comprehensively informative and as attractive as possible. If the school creates its own print materials for teacher recruiting, these should obviously be good-looking and focused on why it's great to teach at St. Basalt's—professional development opportunities, community, programs—and try to differentiate or at least be very specific about the professional and social culture of the school; good photographs showing actual teaching will help. Schools need to remember that the recruiting season is about attracting and energizing smart, committed teachers and not about impressing them with the school's past glories; these matter, but the teacher will be starting work this year and needs to have a sense of what the school is like as a place to work, grow, and live.

Other places to look for potential teachers include such usual suspects as college and university placement offices but also employment fairs with a public/charter school focus (look around or check with your local public school system), industrial employment fairs (there might be some potentially terrific

STEAM teachers who could be curious to sit down with a school at such a fair in times when job pickings are slim), and even local teacher union newsletters. The U.S. government's Troops to Teachers program "helps eligible military personnel begin a new career as teachers." Teachers ending their stints with Teach for America may be good bets, as well.

Although some school administrators detest the hiring process and work to complete it as soon as possible, its importance to the vitality and even viability of the school should inspire creativity, serious effort, and patience. It may take time to bring in "ideal" candidates, but they are out there: expert, diverse, enthusiastic, and excited by the mission of your school. Work thoughtfully to find them and to let them know as much as possible about the school even before beginning to interview and hire, and the next year will go even more smoothly because the new hires will understand and be committed to the school and its mission.

Admirable Faculties, January 14, 2009

14 TWELVE MAXIMS FOR HIRING AND SUSTAINING TEACHERS

"Hiring season" in many schools commences just after the December holiday season comes to an end. Here are a dozen maxims on teacher hiring and care, derived from my 2005 NAIS book, An Admirable Faculty: Recruiting, Hiring, Training, and Retaining Teachers in Independent Schools. The ideas may be old, but they are not, I sincerely believe, dated.

MAXIM #1—Every opening is an opportunity
- No matter how beloved the departed, the new person can be as effective or possibly even more so
- Look at every opening from an institutional point of view—strategic and practical needs
- Even Mr. Chips retired at last; but you are *not* replacing someone, you are *filling a position*

- If your school is already perfect in every way, you don't need this to be reading this anyhow; the wind will just blow Mary Poppins your way

MAXIM #2—Know thyself as an institution and a culture; keep these things in mind:

- Your mission
- Core values
- Who works well in your community
- Your ideals
- Your institutional needs—on a moral and social-emotional level, not just practical
- Your community—what it is, what it is like

MAXIM #3—It takes a school to hire a teacher

- Build a hiring team comprised of more or less the same people/functions for every hire
- Advertise smart
- Interview smart
- Use each candidate as a mirror; what do you learn about the school as your community "presents" itself?

MAXIM #4—You *can* always get what you want

- Advertise smart
- Advertise broadly
- Work hard
- Be patient
- Work harder

Corollary A: Diversity: There is no excuse for failure

- Know what you mean, mean what you say
- A little humility goes a long way
- Advertise smarter
- Work even harder

Corollary B: Cannon fodder: There is no excuse for hiring "expendable" teachers

- You're a school; hire teachers, not just live bodies

- Don't give up before you start; don't hire just to get it over with
- Dorms matter, teams matter, and classes matter—but students matter more
- Be prepared to give people the proper tools to do a proper job
- "Good enough" isn't

MAXIM #5—Check it out

- Check *all* references!
- Do the most thorough background checks you can do; don't let the statutory minimum be good enough
- Got vans? Checking driving records!

MAXIM #6—Induction matters

- Make your initial investment count
- And make an initial investment in time and effort
- Know thyself and bring each new teacher into the learning and living community

Corollary: **There is a reason that Mentor shows up early in *The Odyssey*; make sure your mentors show up early, too**

- It's a tough journey for a new teacher—provide a map and a guide
- Be alert for where your new hires are going to encounter minefields, mind games, and milestones

MAXIM #7—Good teachers can be made

- You MUST believe this
- Provide access, opportunity, and feedback
- More opportunity, more feedback
- Be specific when you are trying to help

MAXIM #8—School culture is everything. Do all that you can to make yours both inviting and welcoming.

- Be a learning community
- Be a civil community

- Be an honest community
- Be a loving community
- Foster cross-generational cross-fertilization

MAXIM #9—Not everybody wants an office

- Administration: not for everyone
- Support ambition, honor commitment, develop real leadership; even your youngest and newest can be leaders
- Not all leaders are administrators, not all administrators are leaders (and not everyone needs to be either)
- But don't stint on providing opportunity

MAXIM #10—Teachers' needs matter

- Tailor-make benefits for all ages and stages
- Be serious about this, and try harder
- Beware the curses that paternalism calls down upon a faculty: dependency, cynicism, complacency

MAXIM #11—Old dogs actually like to learn new tricks

- And they *can* learn them
- Access and opportunity are for everyone
- In a learning community, learning is supposed to be fun and rewarding; is this true with professional learning in your community?

Corollary: But some old dogs like to find their own tricks

- "I don't want to know a trick until I've seen it work"
- But teach a man to fish…
- Bartleby was a lousy employee in the role he was assigned; sometimes it's worth asking what someone might prefer

MAXIM #12—All things must end

- We know about the bad stuff: "cause," "employment at will"; we hear the war stories
- Sometimes it's time: counseling out

- Counsel for growth when you have the opportunity
- Help manage exit strategies for the school and for the teacher; you're a human organization
- Preparing the chute: if it's not good, document, document, document
- Celebrate the Glorious End, but express gratitude in any event; you're a human organization

An awkward cautionary Corollary: **Don't be stupid**

- We've all read the newspaper stories about schools that gently moved problematic teachers along
- Do you want your school in the *Boston Globe*'s "Spotlight"?

A much sweeter (but sometimes extremely bittersweet) Corollary: **Be nicer than you ever thought you could be**

- Sometimes the end comes in the hardest, cruelest way, often unexpected; know how you will honor lives that end in your community
- Whether someone left, retired, or died in harness, they gave a part of their life to your school, your students, and your community. *Honor this in full, and never forget!*

Independent Curriculum Group Blog, December 17, 2018

SUPPORTING TEACHERS

Perspective by Richard Kassissieh, *Assistant Head of School for Academics and Strategic Initiatives, University Prep*

Teacher induction, mentorship, and teaching standards: many schools address these needs somewhat, but few do so thoroughly or with great effectiveness. Since an independent school's faculty is (or should be) its greatest asset, teacher development through a culture of mentorship makes the difference between a school that looks great from a distance and one that actually is great to its students. Peter addresses these topics with nuance and precision. His advice is both pointed and supportive, so listen well!

I learned to listen well to Peter at the Academic Leaders Retreats that he organized. While professional development is a rich industry with hundreds of offerings, Peter's retreats uniquely homed in on the human experience of teaching. "You are probably excited, and probably scared," he writes in "A Letter to New Teachers." Yet, Peter also stayed current, as the same 2014 letter demonstrates in its exploration of educational technologies. While these references may feel dated today, the attention given to the intersection of innovation and school culture is timeless. Peter truly bridges generations.

Peter modeled the retreat after David Mallery's workshops, adding the "fireside chat." While I have found ssome "fireside chats" to forego both fire and chatting, Peter's included both. During these talks, Peter would share thoughts about schools and education today, the work of teachers, and the nature of students and families. The format really suited Peter, with his ability to tell engaging stories and connect seemingly disparate ideas.

In this chapter, dear reader, you get to enjoy the same conversational fire, so close your eyes (between paragraphs) and imagine Peter's deep baritone voice, a crackling fire, and a cold starry night. Then go listen to his podcast on OneSchoolhouse!

15 A LETTER TO NEW TEACHERS

(Note: I originally posted this in July of 2011. It proved to be both popular and durable, and so I revised and re-posted it as the 2014–15 school year approached.)

If it hasn't already, within a very few weeks school will be starting, and you will be starting a wonderful new career.

You are probably excited, and probably scared. A dozen large questions loom in your consciousness, endlessly trading places with one another in the Anxiety Gavotte that troubles the dreams (and waking thoughts, too) even of experienced teachers: Will I know my subject matter? Will I be able to manage my classroom? Will I get along with my new colleagues? Can I have a life and be a teacher, too? Will my school be a good fit for me?

You're entering the profession at an exciting time, as I'm sure you have been told. Technology really is changing everything, and even the methods used by your very best teachers, perhaps just five or six years ago, are undergoing some major changes. Thought leaders in our world call these changes "disruptive," and many of them are just that. It's likely that your school, although they may not have said this in so many words, will be looking to you, who are probably younger and casually adept at thinking about things through a Web 2.0-kind of lens, to quietly set an example for your more senior colleagues.

Speaking of more senior colleagues, there are a couple of things I want to warn you about, but these are things that can really help you grow as a teacher if you handle them the right way.

All this change, this "disruption," is going making school unsettling for some experienced teachers; they're being asked to assemble a whole new toolkit after years of developing their own ways of doing things. They see their schools—their working homes—changing. Some of them are grumpy about this, and sometimes there is cynicism.

Don't stick around to listen or participate; you'll have plenty of other things to do, anyhow. Just walk away—you don't have to chime in or argue, as you'll soon figure out who is worth listening to.

But here's something that you can do to help: When you see a real reason to do so, ask one of the grumps for help or maybe even advice. They won't necessarily make it easy, but in the end they will most likely offer you what you're looking for. After all, what's bothering them is the fear that amid all this change what they DO know isn't going to be valued any more.

What they know that is of value, if they're good enough to have been kept on for a while, is that teaching isn't about content and it's not about technology. It's about kids, about building relationships with them, about believing in them, about finding out what they can do and then providing opportunities for them to do it. And it's about seeing them goof up and giving them chances to try again.

In the end it doesn't matter so much if the approach is Old School—memorize the formula, do grammar exercises 1 through 13, odd—or all about a New Culture of Learning that grows around not-teaching. Know your students, have faith in their capacities, and magical things will happen.

It isn't going to be easy, you know. You might get lucky and have most everything fall into place quickly, but there are probably going to be things you struggle with—perhaps as much as anything you've ever done or even imagined doing.

Here's the thing: You're not as alone—all, all alone—as you will feel. Be in charge of what you can, but when things get really hard, be forthright in taking your worries and concerns to a simpatico colleague or an administrator you trust. (With whom did you click with the best when you were being interviewed? Start there.) Ask someone to sit in on and observe your unruly section or to help you organize your assignments and assessments so that you can actually finish your own homework each night. Whatever it is, you owe it to your students and your school to seek the assistance you need, pronto. And your school owes it to you to help. It's a problem to be solved, and it can be and will be.

I have three last things to offer:

First, you're a professional now, and with that comes some responsibilities. Think of doctors, who spend their lives learning even as they practice. The best teachers do the same, and you should try to emulate that—if for no other reason than to stay on the right side of all the disruptive change that's coming along.

Another responsibility involves being a grown-up. You can like your students, and they can adore you—but you're their teacher, not their best buddy, their secret-sharer, or their guru. If you need to score points off the adulation of kids, you might want to quit teaching and become a celebrity. Otherwise, earn your students' trust and their respect, which will serve you, and them, a whole lot better in the long run.

Second, parents. Yup, lots of them are hovering these days, and they can be kind of hard to take sometimes.

The deal is, parents are the way they are because they love their kids. I'm afraid that most of us parents screw it up pretty regularly, and I'm sure I've made my kids' teachers' eyes roll. But in the end the strongest teachers are very good at gently, and sometimes not so gently, reminding parents that we're all on the same side here. So plan on spending some time figuring out how to help parents and guardians understand the common purpose. And it helps to remember that sometimes teachers are actually wrong.

Lastly, before your orientation begins and the whirlwind of opening weeks sucks all the idealistic notions out of your head for a while, go to your school's website or your handbook and re-read the mission statement. If there are sections on values and history, read those, too.

Because teaching is a profession of ideals. Somebody founded your school because they believed in something worthy, and the school has evolved in certain ways because of those beliefs. Sometimes the beliefs get lost, sometimes they get transmogrified, and occasionally a school has had to stop and then start all over again in a new direction. But believe me, worthy beliefs are fundamental to the enterprise.

You're about to become a living exemplar of those beliefs. Whenever you rise to your best in the classroom, at lunch, on the field, in the dorm, or in the faculty room, you are in some way going to embody the mission of your school. Sometimes you may have to squint to see it, and you may have to take a leap of faith every now and then, but don't forget it—or let others forget it, either.

So: Believe in kids, soften up your crusty colleagues, be a grown-up, be patient with parents, and, to paraphrase a much better man than I, be the mission you wish to see in the world.

Also: Don't forget to breathe. And have fun, lots of it.

Not Your Father's School, July 21, 2014

16 INDUCTION AND ORIENTATION FOR NEW TEACHERS

By now our new teachers are in at least in the second weeks of school, and we like to think that they are settling in comfortably.

Experience, however, suggests that many are still in something resembling panic mode: student work is piling up, conferences and parent/guardian events are looming, and they are holding onto their curricula by the skin of their chattering teeth. Each day brings its little pleasures, but it also brings the possibility of stepping on one of the little landmines with which school cultures seem inevitably to be littered.

More and more schools have introduced some kind of mentoring program, but the multitude of things that new teachers must learn are often left to trial and error. In the old days—my old days, at least, now long ago—new teachers had about an hour's head start on the veterans before opening faculty meetings began, and the on-the-job training that accompanied the first weeks in a new school was supposed to toughen us (if anyone thought about it at all). Most schools are doing better than this, but I'm a big fan of serious, thoughtful, and detailed induction and orientation programs.

Maybe the horse is too far out of the barn by now, at least for this school year, but I think the essential elements of a great program that really prepares teachers for life in a new school include:

- ✓ *"Electronic induction"*—giving new teachers access as soon as possible after hiring to the school email system and other important digital resources that will be essential to his or her life and work; this would absolutely include a curriculum map, if the school maintains one
- ✓ *Pre-service inclusion*—making sure that new hires are included in any summer meetings or planning sessions that will be in any way relevant to their work

- ✓ *Access to texts and materials*—delivering to the teacher early on any textbooks or other teaching materials that he or she will be using
- ✓ *Access to handbooks and manuals*—delivering to the teacher any student or employee handbooks that would help explain the culture and policies of the school; I would modestly recommend ***The Teacher's Guide to Life and Work***, available as a free download from One Schoolhouse (currently among the [resources on the Independent Curriculum Pages](). The Guide is presented as a fully editable doc with lots of placeholder content that is both generic and likely to be relevant. Download, and edit away!)
- ✓ *An orientation program that focuses on school culture and values, unique aspects of the instructional program, and lots of "nuts & bolts"*—no opportunity to introduce new faculty to key people in the school community, including students and parents/guardians, should be lost
- ✓ *Dedicated guided prep time*—giving the teacher the opportunity to develop lesson plans and activities for the first days and weeks of school by working directly with a mentor, co-teacher, or department leader
- ✓ *A mentor*, or at least a close contact whose experience has been similar to the new teacher's, and who will be working geographically near the new teacher during the year

The school that is willing to take the time and trouble to support a program that includes these elements and works hard to see that they are well implemented will have gone a long way toward easing the transition of new teachers. If the program has the elegantly simple goal of eliminating surprise from new teachers' lives, those little landmines we all remember can be reduced to mild bumps that are part of a gentle acclimation process rather than an unpredictable series of terrifying or demoralizing jolts.

Admirable Faculties, September 18, 2008

17 A CULTURE OF MENTORSHIP

Well, school's not quite ready to start, but I am, and it's time to start thinking about how schools can build faculty competencies and do a better job at that thing we are supposed to do. Our new faculty members just completed a three-day program to hone their differentiation chops, and this afternoon the big work starts: they meet with their department heads to start working on and reviewing their curriculum and lesson plans for the first month of school, followed by three more days of sessions on school culture and procedures. Last week we also handed them their hard copies of the *Teacher's Guide to Life and Work*; they have been able to access this through our new teacher wiki since July.

We focus on making the orientation program into a real immersion into school culture. The program tomorrow starts with an in-depth, anecdotal school tour where we meet administrators and otherwise see the school from the inside out; we even have a session just on the odd lingo our school uses. (QUICK HINT FOR MAKING THE NEW YEAR A SUCCESS FOR NEW TEACHERS: Start making a little glossary of the idiosyncratic terms for your own school, and see how quickly you need to add pages.)

By the time it's all over, all the new faculty in both divisions will have met a pretty good range of their colleagues as well as people in administrative functions that bear on their work directly and indirectly, and so when full faculty meetings start next week no one will feel like a stranger.

For the past couple of years we have de-emphasized the artificial "here's your mentor/blind date" thing. Great mentorship programs are built from the ground up and cost serious money when you start easing teaching loads for mentors and new folks and trying to schedule common planning time; I'm all for programs like this, but most schools, particularly in a tough economy, can't afford them. Instead, what we have been aiming for is a "CULTURE OF MENTORSHIP," in which department chairs, divisional and departmental colleagues, class deans, and others in a position to do so understand the needs of each new cohort of teachers and pick up the reins *constantly* to check in, observe, offer feedback, help, support, and guide the new people into the fabric of the faculty's professional life.

Building a culture of mentorship requires that we be especially explicit and intentional about this. Each group that meets—department chairs, deans—needs to be reminded that "it takes a village to make a teacher successful." It turns out that each previous year's new teacher cohort can be helpful here, too, and we debrief with them pretty regularly throughout their first year. Last year our new teachers took a couple of afternoon retreats with a small group of what we call Lead Teachers—teachers who have piloted program ideas and who have become an important in-house professional development resource for all faculty.

The worry, of course, is that a teacher here or an issue there might slip through the cracks, and we have to keep working on how we do this. But I think that overall the model has some real advantages over the old "blind date" model, which sometimes worked out very well but just as often fizzled after the first couple of weeks. I think that all the pre-service work that we do really contributes to success, as no teacher enters our building without a really good grounding not only in the professional and educational culture of the school but also in the critical "who's who" questions: *Where do I go for help? What can I expect from (that person or that office)?* This matters a great deal.

I still hear stories of schools with half-day orientations for new teachers, or where the half-day program is proudly announced to have become a full day. I don't think that is anywhere near enough time or enough exposure to key people and key roles to truly "orient" a new teacher. I worry that one-on-one mentorship programs added to over-short orientations serve more to isolate new teachers or create a sense of urgent dependency than to give them the confidence and basic knowledge they will need to succeed from Day One.

A culture of mentorship is really another term for a professional learning community, and it would be nice to think that all of our schools would be focused on creating this kind of environment and culture for their faculties. In the meantime, we have to work hard to build in the structures (where we can) and the intention (everywhere) to make coming into a new school as seamless and as success-focused as possible.

Admirable Faculties, August 24, 2009

18 FEEDBACK FOR NEW TEACHERS

I just finished writing up a precis of my check-in conversations with all our new faculty, and I am giving ourselves a big pat on the back not only for a program that has so far kept these good people free from huge surprises but also for having done two things pretty thoughtfully and, it appears, well.

The first is hiring. Our main thrust for many years has been to find people who are really well matched in values and skills not just with our subject-matter teaching needs but with our school. The administrators who do this read lots of folders, talk to many, many candidates, and engage in a very intentional process of informed consent with finalists. We don't shy from telling people what is hard about working at our school—mainly the need to be passionate about and attentive to both students and the craft of teaching—as well as what the rewards are.

The second is a kind of full-court press of support. The new teachers have all been in department meetings and divisional meetings in which the subject is pedagogy and best practices, and they have all been visited by now by both a department head and a division head. These are not formal evaluative observations but rather opportunities for administrators to understand the classroom cultures that are forming and to offer warm feedback and input based on what is observed.

As a school we seem to be moving hopefully toward what I would call an open-door policy, where colleagues and academic administrators are in and out of one another's classrooms all the time, normalizing the "adult in the back of the room" as a friendly part of the landscape of a learning community.

All I can think of is my first years of teaching. In the first school, no administrator or supervisor entered the building where I taught, much less my classroom; my close friend who taught in the classroom next to me was in and out of my classroom, as I was in and out of his. Together we moved by trial and error toward what felt like but may not have been competence. I'm still in the biz, but he left after a year. In my second school a walkabout head poked his face into my room pretty regularly, but only once did I receive direct issue-related feedback and only once, in my third year, was I formally observed, in response to a "problem" (which was easily and painlessly solved). The next school was about the same, as was my current school for the first eight or nine years I was here.

Steve Clem, of AISNE and "Eloquent Mirrors" fame, likes to point out that he might have been a much better teacher much earlier in his career if he had received feedback on his work, and I feel this just as acutely. We serve our teachers badly and our students even more badly when we don't do everything we can, not just to give teachers the materials they need and goals to meet but also immediate, regular, and clear feedback on their work that will help them realize their potential as educators as quickly as possible.

It seems quite silly (and worse) in retrospect when schools fail to make an early and positive effort to make sure that the new teachers they are at such pains to hire are both comfortable in their work and given the real, immediate feedback—on curriculum, on classroom management, on professionalism—they need to take their work to the highest level.

So if you are an administrator reading this, check in with your new faculty soon. Drop into their classrooms, find out how things are going, and let them know how you think things are going, based on some real observation. It's never too early to start, but after a while it may be too late.

Admirable Faculties, September 23, 2008

19 MAKING TEACHERS

It's been noted before, but one difference between many independent schools and the public system has to do with the development of teachers. It's an area in which some readers may believe that the vaunted world of private education has feet of clay, but it's worth talking about.

Teacher development happens to be something near and dear to me. I've written books about it, spoken about it, and been involved at various levels with the work itself. I know that systematic training is far better than the initial sort of preparation I received: faith in my college degrees, a pile of textbooks, a box of chalk, and lots of on-the-run advice.

In time, I went through the process of becoming certified, coursework I happen to look back on quite fondly as having influenced my practice in good ways. Had public schools in Massachusetts been hiring in 1978, I might be writing this from another perspective entirely.

I will also stipulate that more and more of the teacher candidates and early career teachers I encounter—in fact, virtually all of those in early childhood, elementary, and middle school classrooms—are fully certified teachers. It still seems understood that the best preparation for teaching fundamental skills to younger students is a good teacher-training course, either at the undergraduate or—for career-changers, of whom we see more than a few (why, I'm even married to one)—graduate level.

Teachers of older children in independent schools, however, come from more varied backgrounds and enter the profession with more diverse professional needs. Certified teachers, often ex-public school (here an ironic "thank you" to the educational budget cutters who have put these often outstanding educators on the market) are not thin on the ground, but the preponderance, I would venture, enter the field with undergraduate majors and graduate degrees in the subjects they teach. (A few teachers land in independent schools from Teach for America, which I know will seem problematic for some readers—although these teachers have at least remained in the profession.)

The good news is that many schools are onto the needs of inexperienced teachers. Induction and orientation programs are generally longer than the half day that started me nearly 40 years back, and many schools have developed mentoring programs with real substance. Furthermore, administrators and supervisors know that assiduous hand-holding, close observation, and other kinds of personal and professional support are in order for newer teachers; increasingly, the school's responsibility to provide this is built into evaluation systems that focus on teachers in what some public schools might consider the "pre-tenure" period of employment.

One might be tempted to scoff at the apparent irony that parents are paying tens of thousands of dollars to have their children taught by teachers with little or no professional experience or training, and it's certainly a reality. Another reality, though, is that independent school teachers tend to exist within cultures that are highly immersive: in 21st-century independent schools it is hard for a new or newish teacher not to be constantly watched, engaged in conversations about practice and about kids, and otherwise offered a great deal of formal and informal on-the-job training from a number of experienced sources. Generally smaller classes and relatively small and intense school communities make it relatively easy for intentional schools to monitor and offer essentially real-time feedback to early-career teachers.

Another phenomenon on the rise is that of regional training programs for aimed at cohorts of new teachers, ranging from pre-service bootcamps to series of formal meetings and workshops that extend throughout the school year, perhaps supplemented by a weekend retreat or two.

Also worth mentioning are the growing number of "apprenticeship" programs that couple school-based internships with formal coursework toward a teaching degree as well as certification. The oldest of these, to my knowledge, is offered by Shady Hill School in Cambridge, Massachusetts, but similar paths are available elsewhere. The Klingenstein Center at Teachers College of Columbia University offers master's programs in educational leadership among its many programs aimed at independent school educators at all career stages; Johns Hopkins, Mount Holyoke, and a handful of other universities offer programs leading to industry-recognized credentials in educational leadership—often tied to degree programs.

Other programs offer training minus the state credential. Some schools offer internship/apprenticeship programs on their own, and there is the Progressive Education Lab program, a moveable feast of experiences.

I suppose the flip side of the sometimes uneven preparation level of some independent school teachers is that we're also bombarded these days by evidence, or at least opinion couched as evidence, that many college teacher training programs leave something to be desired. I have no opinion to offer here; my own experience (as a student, a colleague, and as a parent of kids taught by certified teachers) was certainly the opposite, but I cannot generalize from that.

What I can say is that schools have a pretty good idea and are learning more every day about what it takes to develop effective teachers. Much of it goes back to fundamentals: a good brain, a very good heart, a passion for the work, and a commitment to the success of kids. A big chunk is about fit—do the teacher's values, methods, and ambitions match those of the school and its community? All of these, I think, are universals in all sectors, and go well beyond a piece of paper in a new teacher's hand.

The most effective and successful schools understand deeply that developing outstanding teachers and faculties of lifelong professional learners is every bit as important as their work with students. I see more schools thinking ever more intentionally about the training and support of newer teachers and the ongoing professional learning of veterans. If we are to claim to be schools that have a broader and higher purpose than churning out happy graduates, attending to the skills and professionalism of our teachers must be at the center of our work.

"Independent Schools, Common Perspectives," *Education Week*, May 17, 2013

20 TEACHING STANDARDS

We hear a great deal about classroom standards, but there is another set of standards that we've heard both more and less about. The media and the politicians are all in a sweat about "higher standards for teachers," but relatively few schools have gone out of their way to state what these standards are.

In independent schools there has long been a prideful sense that we know good teaching when we see it, and this is probably sometimes true. What is harder though, and what may have been doing our students harm over the years, is that many of our schools have not made explicit our standards for good teaching; when teachers have been dismissed or eased out, it has more often been for "cause"—an egregious mistake or act—or because they have been gently counseled out: something in the quality of their work has been deficient, and they are unwelcome. The match is bad, they are told, and they are urged to find greener pastures. In the meantime, some of their perhaps only slightly better colleagues stay on, doing work that is just good enough. Everyone may know who these teachers are, but the administration doesn't have the right mechanisms—or perhaps the will, in a culture of benign neglect—to tell these teachers specifically how to improve their practice.

A few years back I sat in a workshop on observing teaching conducted by my friend Steve Clem. On the connection between observation and evaluation, Steve made the wry comment, "Of course your teachers are evaluated against specific standards; all your schools have generated their own Standards for Effective Teaching, right?" A roomful of educational leaders from some of the finest schools in the region (just ask us) looked hard at their shoes. By the time I was back at school that afternoon, however, I'd decided that creating such standards at our place would be a worthy and perhaps not so complicated project, and that having them in place might make it a whole lot easier to frame both an evaluation system that was then a work in progress and an increasingly elaborate and intentional professional development program.

The process of generating our standards turned out to be not so hard, and the language of our standards has become the basis for the formal "rubric" part of our evaluation system as well as part of the conceptual framework (that also includes our mission statement) on which our professional development and individual professional growth efforts are based.

I get to work with a few schools here and there that are interested in professional development, evaluation, and building new and sustaining kinds of professional cultures. The work I do is usually pretty fundamental, and I always leave them with the suggestion that developing standards for effective teaching would be a pretty great next step. It's not that hard, I tell them, but I think for faculties unused to being well and consistently evaluated in their work or treated to engaging and intentional professional development, it looks like a daunting task.

But generating standards for effective teaching in a mission-based, thoughtful school really isn't that hard, and I think that any school that needs to explain its own standards, either in the marketplace or within its own walls, ought to make the effort. Teachers who have a clear understanding of what is expected of them are liberated by this clarity, and those who want to grow and improve—and experience shows that most teachers want this very much—can focus on specific and even measurable ways to do this. Schools with clear standards can also help all teachers grow and avoid the tragedy of barely satisfactory teachers who never quite cross the line into "cause" but who yet are never shown how improve—faculty members whose classrooms become limbos not just for these teachers but for their inadequately served students.

If you recognized yourself among those educators looking at the floor when the subject of Standards for Effective Teaching was raised, there's never a better time than now to contemplate a process for developing your school's own. Whether you start from scratch or base yours on existing models (the National Board for Professional Teaching Standards has a great deal to say on this), a set of such standards can be a starting point for some great work in the development of great faculties.

It also occurs to me that all kinds of schools can do themselves a big favor in the public eye by developing and publishing their standards for good teaching. They should then make sure that teachers are held to these standards and given opportunities to excel in them so that the best of them become true master teachers who can lead their faculties from within even as they exemplify the school's very best work.

When parents, politicians, and pundits are confident that teachers are doing the best work they can be against known benchmarks of real performance rather than externally applied measures that make little or no sense, schools and teachers will be given the support they need and the respect they deserve.

Admirable Faculties, October 4, 2008

THE TEACHING LIFE

Perspective by Elise London, *Head of Upper School,*
Moses Brown School
In the posts that follow, Peter Gow urges us to examine our commitment as educators to "hone one's own craft." He provides a number of road maps and suggestions to help us along this journey—as he parses the ways we can become "All-Terrain Teachers," questions the ways we define the "whole child," challenges us to see all students as future success stories, and encourages us all to stay true to our authentic and individual selves in the classroom. It is Peter's belief in teaching as a craft to be honed, rather than simply as a job to be done, that makes him such an exemplary leader and gives him such a vision to support school change. As he writes, we all need to "master the art of moving forward amid ever-shifting conditions"—conditions that are both within our schools and our students but also reflected in the changing world around us.

Schools don't exist in a vacuum, but, rather, they reflect the world as it is. Peter knows this all too well. In the years we worked together in the Independent Curriculum Group, Peter and I got to ask the hard questions about school change and help school leaders envision the answers. We got to champion schools that worked to provide vigorous, school-specific, curriculum where the answers did not come on a standardized test and the curriculum did not come out of a package. Schools would seek Peter's wisdom, as reflected in these posts, as he led faculty conversations about how to balance change, and he soothed the fears of those who worried that leaving AP behind would mean losing students, applicants, teachers, and rigor. Peter was right at the forefront of that moment, honing his own craft to adapt his teaching to our ever-shifting landscape. It's been an honor and a privilege to get to work beside, but often one step behind, him, following the path he has forged.

21   THE ALL-TERRAIN TEACHER

Things are getting rugged in the fall of 2008, and change is in the wind.

But a few things are becoming more clear for educators. One obvious fact is that the diversity train has left the station in our society. No matter who becomes the next president, some things in our country and on our continent are changing, and those of us who teach kids had better be ready. I keep hearing predictions as to when "Whites in the U.S. will be a minority"—2020, 2050; it doesn't much matter, because it is the future.

But when will this racial and cultural diversity be manifest everywhere? Not regionally, not city/suburb, not public school/private school, but everywhere we go and everywhere we look and everywhere we live. Sadly, I think the date when this is likely to happen is bit farther off, as the majority has become quite adept at keeping to itself when it's in our (*ouch!* but yes, it's my truth) interest to do so.

If independent schools are as committed as most of them say they are to issues of equity and justice, and if they really want to enact the ideals in their missions, they have some work to do. Lots of our schools are busy doing that work, discovering that the farther along they get, the harder the work becomes. Idealism of any sort requires great courage and great honesty, and humans are frail; when having to open our minds and our hearts to whole new ways of being and knowing, we are often more frail still.

A few years ago a colleague by the name of Nadine Nelson did some amazing work at our school, helping us figure out how to be a better place for our students and colleagues from underrepresented groups. She had a term that has stayed with me, the "all-terrain kid." The ATK was the student who would be sufficiently curious, sufficiently self-aware, sufficiently humble, sufficiently informed, and sufficiently brave to be at home in any cultural milieu. Parachute the All-Terrain Kid into any setting, and they would be able to present themself with respect and intelligence and to communicate on an authentic level with anyone.

The All-Terrain Kid is an ideal I still hold in my head for our students and for my own children. That's the kid who won't care about a whole lot of things that agitate our society now, and for whom newly evolving communities that truly represent the diversity of our society and our planet will be welcome, exciting places.

I think schools should be thinking equally hard about developing the All-Terrain Teacher. However one construes "diversity," the ATT has to be able to negotiate it with the integrity, wit, and courage in all of its manifestations. Who is going to teach a generation of All-Terrain Kids, if not a generation of All-Terrain Teachers?

A while back TJX Corporation put together a diversity task force build around what they called the "arenas of diversity." As strange as the source may seem, I like the model, and drawing on it I would propose that the training and the work of the All-Terrain Teacher be built around these **Five Arenas of Diversity**:

- ✓ **Age and generation.** We've become cutely adept at naming generations and fractions of generations to differentiate them, but differentiation cannot become segregation. Boomers, Millennials, or whatever—they will represent significant diversity in an aging society paradoxically built around youth culture, and they will need to learn to understand one another and work together. This is especially true in schools, where the (relatively) old and the (relatively) young must come together for the highest of common purposes

- ✓ **Race and culture.** Whatever the other dimensions of diversity, these remain at the heart of the matter. Often visible and burdened with a long and terrible history, race matters, and so, broadly construed, does culture, especially in a society dogged by its own identity crisis, as witnessed by the fact that millions of people can seriously ask the question, *Is Barack Obama really American?* and by a dangerous national ambivalence on the issue of immigration.

- ✓ **Gender and sexual orientation.** How do we build a society that can guarantee security, respect, and equal opportunity and reward to all people, regardless of gender, gender expression, and sexual identity? Schools are already unsafe places for children who wrestle with these issues, and the achievement gap between the binaries of "boy" and "girl" seems to be growing. These challenges must be addressed, and as always, schools are the crucibles in which better practices must be forged.

- ✓ **Class and status.** We've been living through an era when income disparities have risen to all-time highs and when "Masters of the Universe" privilege themselves in every conceivable way. At the same time, the "middle class" scarcely knows how to define itself. Teachers and especially selective, tuition-driven schools are going to have to face difficult issues in this arena.

- ✓ **Ability and wellness.** Issues around health care, accessibility, genetic testing, and accommodation of different abilities will continue to grow as genetic science moves forward and as our society ages. How will differences in access to services and support manifest themselves among students and teachers, and how will schools be able to confidently address these differences? Will schools have to take stands on issues we cannot now even foresee?

The All-Terrain Teacher in the thoughtful school will need to have given enormous intentional consideration to each of these areas. Some schools may choose to opt out of this work, keeping their doors and hearts closed to certain kinds of difference, but the terrain that their students, families, and faculties will be negotiating will change nonetheless. Those who choose not to participate will surely be left far behind.

Like the All-Terrain Kid, the All-Terrain Teacher is an ideal. But the ideal can be fulfilled. It will take more than workshops and seminars, more than "diversity days" and diversity offices. It will have to begin with a systemic acknowledgment within the school that the world is truly changing, and that old modes and orders are going to be giving way to new and more just ones, regardless of anyone's comfort with the change. To do the work will take nerves of steel and a willingness both to try new things and to learn from our blunders as we do.

Perhaps there is a Sixth Arena of Diversity, the arena of change itself. Above all, schools that want to be "all-terrain" will need to master the art of moving forward like a camel in a sandstorm, amid ever-shifting conditions and the ever-present temptation to stop and rest. The goal, a world whose ideals reflect the loftiest ideals of the school, is out there, right where our words and our hopes have placed it. If we just keep it in sight, we can make it through the most rugged of times.

Admirable Faculties, October 24, 2008

22 WHATEVER OUR PASSIONS, THERE IS A TIME TO BE STILL AND LISTEN

Every now and then I am overcome by guilt over my own role in this echo chamber of the blogosphere. I'm as guilty as the next guy of (un?-)helpfully providing lists of "11 Things Your School Has to Be Thinking About"; it's a bit about arrogance (I'll own it), a bit about grandstanding (I'll confess to that, too). In my case it is also a simple wish, for deeply felt reasons, that all schools might live up to their ideals and provide experiences precisely consonant with the promises they imply by their missions.

What are the reasons? Here goes.

When I was a wee laddie my family was in the school biz. I never had even an inkling that any of the adults around me wanted to do less than support and help every single one the kids at the family school. I saw a lot of grown-ups doing a lot of worrying, some of it about enrollment and the bills, but a whole lot more of it about how to do a good job for Barry or Judd or Donald or Randy—the kids for whom the school was going to be, hopefully, the last stop before college, college being a place none of these dyslexic boys' previous schools had ever thought they could get to. I ate a lot of TV dinners waiting for my father to come home from dinner, from faculty meetings, or from just checking in with his students in evening study hall. If I didn't eat it with him in the school dining hall, I didn't breakfast with my father, ever.

The school was small and unadorned and so was its mission, and I had a front-row seat at the show as Mission: Impossible became Mission: Accomplished for a couple of dozen seniors every year.

I was hooked on the life from an early age, and I read everything I could about schools and how they worked. The glossy school catalogues and newspapers that arrived in the mail regularly were my comic books, and a slightly out-of-date *Porter Sargent Handbook of Private Schools* was my bible. I've been a sucker for "prep school" novels since discovering *Good-Bye, Mr. Chips* in my grandfather's bookcase, and A *Separate Peace* made me hurt when I first read it (and still does).

I believe in independent schools the way Bostonians believe in the Red Sox, and I want these schools to be the best. When I was younger this manifested itself in preppy arrogance of the worst kind, and I owe the world an apology for that. By the time I was settled in as a real teacher—and I had to run away from home at the start of my career to accomplish this on my own terms—I came to realize that being the best isn't about winning, it's about being the best version of oneself, living up to all of one's ideals and hopes and aspirations. This, I realized a while back, is what I want for independent schools.

Independent School Nation, to push the Boston baseball metaphor, is made up of schools and educators and students and parents and students for whom I have the highest of expectations. Just as I want every at-bat for Big Papi to be a home run and every inning Koji pitches to be immaculate, I want every teacher to be energized and skilled, every coach a paragon, every head a leader of wisdom and compassion, every school a place of justice and mercy, and every word spoken in or about any school to be true. I want students awash in opportunities to embrace and assimilate ideals until each and every one becomes the very best possible version of themselves, and I want our communities to give each student the gifts of circumspection, fair-mindedness, and generosity of spirit so that they can be part of this saving-the-world project we are all embarked upon.

It's not about being better, or truer, or wiser than other people in other kinds of schools; it's not about being exemplary, because that's arrogance, too. It's simply about living up, in our little closed communities, to what we say we want to be, to what our missions and values statements and visions and strategic plans all promise. This is a responsibility we have to ourselves, and to our society. Along the way we need to find enough humility to fall into real conversation with our peers in other sectors—because those sectors have their own believers, folks as great and as accomplished as, say, Deborah Meier, and because those sectors are responsible for a lot more kids than we are.

So that's why I occupy this space, and that's why I tolerate and even join in when the preaching begins.

I have had some role in moving an actual school from survival mode to a growth mindset, imbuing a faculty with a new sense of their own capacities amid an abundance of new ideas and resources. I've listened as the students doing unsupervised group work in the hallway workspace outside my office door moved from being maybe 40% on task to more than 80% on task, a transition just a few years in the making and the greatest single affirmation of a new culture of teaching and learning that I can imagine. I've watched as a school guided only by the simplest of tech "visions"—a set of basic criteria for deciding which way to go—ramped up a transformative 1:1 BYOL program in less than a calendar year. I've been in charge of bidding adieu to a school's last Advanced Placement-designated courses and then having the pleasure, as a college counselor, of explaining our school and successfully advocating for an amazing corps of students to colleges that some feared would be skeptical of AP-less transcripts.

I know, in other words, that change works. I know that wrapping a school's programs and practices around principles based on contemporary understandings of what kids need and what kids can do can take teachers and schools to undreamt-of places, both in terms of basic things like reputation and advancement and in terms of real educational possibilities.

Sometimes, though, I think we all need to shut up, including me. I think we need neither to add nor attend to the hectoring of our twitter feeds and our PLNs but instead to listen to the still, small voices within ourselves and, better still, to the voices of our students and our colleagues as they wrestle with growing and supporting one another and figuring out how it all goes together. We need to remind ourselves of what we believe in and to understand how all of this makes a full, big picture in, and of, our lives.

Not Your Father's School, March 14, 2014

23 DEFINING, THEN SERVING, THE WHOLE CHILD

Somewhere back in the last century educators latched onto a term that makes everyone feel good: "educating the whole child."

Thousands of schools have been built, or re-built, around this theme, and teachers take enormous and deserved pride in seeing themselves as serving the needs of the "whole child" in their classrooms.

I'm not enough of a scholar of the history of childhood to correlate understandings of the meaning of the "whole child" to evolving ideas of childhood's place within our culture. My guess is that the notion of the whole child emerged more or less contemporaneously with Progressive social concepts like curbing child labor and an expanding understanding of "child welfare"—the idea that kids were not just short, cheap-to-hire mini-adults but rather growing organisms whose cognitive, emotional, social, and physical development required specific kinds of attention and nurturance. Equally progressive educational ideas gave us the idea that schools should provide these.

In the 1960s and early 70s a great national project was undertaken to identify and describe the characteristics of children, or for that matter of humans in general. In proper scientific manner, the researchers leading this project—Benjamin Bloom's name is forever attached to its results—tried to break down these characteristics in ways that would be helpful to educators and others interested in child development.

Bloom's Taxonomy identifies three "domains" of learning within which behavioral characteristics and learning objectives could be further broken down. The cognitive domain involves knowledge and thinking, the affective domain encompasses feelings/emotions, and the psychomotor domain involves physical and spatial capacities.

It occurs to me that the heyday of the kind of work that Bloom was leading came to a thudding halt about 30 years ago this past month, with the publication of *A Nation at Risk*. The anxieties expressed were not about how kids felt or how they moved. The emphasis was all on cognition, on the mastery (or not) of classroom content. Fifteen years later we had No Child Left Behind, and now we scrap recess so that kids can do better on bubble tests.

Teachers and schools have done all they could to keep a proportionate amount of their attention on the affective and psychomotor domains, but at some risk. Worry too loudly about how kids are feeling, and you are sneeringly dismissed as being part of the weak-kneed "Self-Esteem Movement." Kids' bodies? It's either all about sports ("If she works hard for the next five years my kid's gonna get a full ride to the U for soccer!") or obesity.

But as a teacher I've worried about both. As an advisor and the past coach of interscholastic teams in a couple of sports, I think I've had plenty of opportunity to participate in "whole child" education—at four very different schools. I'm not alone; most of us, if not all of us, have spent our lives doing the same. Teaching the whole child, attending to our students' development in all kinds of ways, is what good teachers do, and creating conditions where this can happen is what schools intend to do, however they may be distracted by external emphases on other things.

(Parenthetically, if I were going to revisit Bloom's project I might consider, especially in light of what we now see as the skills and habits of mind essential for success in the 21st-century world, adding a fourth domain. I'd back the idea of a "Social Domain," which touches and incorporates bits of the Cognitive, Affective, and Psychomotor but has its own definable characteristics and developmental steps. I'm not entirely sure I can present these as tidily as Bloom and Company presented theirs, but I see significant differences in the ways that kids respond to the social situations at various ages that are both differentiated and predictable as part of developmental and learning trajectories.

Think of the ways children are in school, with friends out of sight of adults, with parents, with strangers, with grandparents, with parents' adult friends—and consider the moment, which seems to come around age 15 or so, when kids discover that a certain kind of behavior will get them taken seriously by adults. All of this, observed and tagged, might help teachers guide students toward becoming more effective leaders, collaborators, citizens, and even creators. But that's just me. You could probably make a case for a Spiritual Domain, as well.)

I guess, though, when I hear the term "whole child" these days that I'm not always sure that my understanding—and I'll make a claim to including everything from kids' very individual brains and hearts and bodies to their connections with family, community, and tradition—is quite what others have in mind. I hope it is, but somehow I can't equate an emphasis merely on the detailed enumerations of standards represented by the Common Core or on multiple-choice tests (and teaching geared toward them) with any reasonably whole children I know.

It's a big world out there, and life is complicated and surprising. "Whole child" education as I understand it intends to prepare children as best we can for all of this. I wonder whether the masterminds devising educational policy in think tanks or campaign strategy sessions really get this.

And then I wonder whether they even want this.

"Independent Schools, Common Perspectives," *Education Week*, May 10, 2013

24   BUSY-NESS

Education has changed in the past few decades, and one indicator of this seems to be that we are all busier than ever. The start of each school year feels more like a scramble, with new initiatives, new ideas, new constraints, and of course new students. My father, who retired as a head nearly 20 years ago and who ran his school with an administrative leanness that is scarcely imaginable today, has a very hard time wrapping his head around the idea that teachers and administrators seem to have so many meetings. "What are you meeting about?" he asks, in an accusatory tone. Are we noisily tailoring new clothes for the emperor only so we look busy and important? Are we only working to out-guilt each other with our claims to be working under barely tolerable loads of stress?

On bad days I think he might be onto something, but on the whole I am confident that the work that good educators are doing these days is pretty substantial. One of the main characteristics of the New Progressivism is an almost fanatical commitment to the re-examination and continuous improvement of practice. If we are meeting more often than our forebears, it is because we are at last talking with one another about the work we do and testing our assumptions and our actions against principles and benchmarks that we are working to make explicit and alive.

I spent an hour yesterday morning sitting with a couple of department chairs and our assistant head of school talking about "units." We're going to make unit design the focus of both our professional development efforts and our acountability system this year, and so we need to establish some baseline language and baseline expectations with which teachers can do the work we will be asking them to do. It was a great conversation, ranging from the challenge of creating great essential questions to the feasibility of integrating some Understanding by Design and Teaching for Understanding concepts into a schematic diagram that would help teachers conceptualize a process at which most are already, in their individual ways, quite adept.

The biggest issue we had, however, was how to present these ideas in ways that will not overwhelm and discourage a faculty already working very, very hard. The trick is to help teachers integrate new understandings into their work in a way that reflects what the Coalition of Essential Schools calls "unanxious expectations"—the idea that we work toward our best not in the hysterical and destructively competitive pursuit of abstract "excellence" but rather by acting calmly and in the service of explicit standards directed toward deep understanding and profound engagement. We have to allow our teachers time and space to build new concepts into their work in a way that is organic and authentic, and we have to give them tools and training to do this well.

A major difference between older models and New Progressivist schools, I like to tell people, is that in our kinds of schools we are asking teachers to take on two jobs. The first is the day-to-day teaching, correcting, advising, and coaching that all teachers must do. The second is the professional work required both to hone one's own craft as well as to forward the aims and strategic goals of the division, the department, and the school. When I was interviewing candidates I called my description of these two tasks the "informed consent" part of the meeting. For a teacher interested in disappearing into a classroom in September to emerge only in June, the New Progressivism is a bad match.

So let's step back, here in late September, to ask ourselves whether our busy lives are worth it in terms of educational expertise expanded and student experience improved. I think that in schools committed to institutional reflection, collaboration, and improvement, all the meetings, all the conversations, all the drafts and redrafts, and finally all the new and better ways of doing the work are more than payoff enough.

I'd go so far as to suggest that the modeling that teachers do in such schools has a powerful effect on our students. In a school where they don't sense complacency and self-satisfaction but rather steady efforts to improve, kids learn that good enough is always just a starting place. Rather than "stressing" students, this understanding becomes internalized as an ethic of improvement and even craftsmanship that will serve them well beyond their years with us.

The New Progressive, September 27, 2008

25 SITTING DOWN TO TURKEY IN DISCOMFORT WITH MY PRIVILEGE

Our epitaph will no doubt be that we were good people, nice people, who tried to do the right thing. Once a year we were even thankful, unless of course we were on an early morning shopping spree or being forced to work selling gadgets and gewgaws at "discount" prices to people who could barely afford them—the ones on the shopping sprees, hoping desperately that overpriced gifts for their loved ones could assuage the pain caused by the economic trap that had been sprung on them by moguls who would later be enjoying their own Thanksgivings over fine wines in gated communities far from the strip malls and big box stores.

It's hard for me to write today; things look pretty bleak in the land despite the fact that I and my family are able to live in some comfort on the margins of an industry largely predicated on the wealth of some, if not others. A week ago I was giving the ritual induction speech for my school's honor society, a little oration that includes the line "justice is slow, and at times just plain absent." I hoped this week that this phrase, which has been ringing especially loudly in my ears of late, is echoing in the heads of the high-achieving students we enrolled as well as in those of their families, peers, and teachers.

Seldom have I felt more alienated from the structures that run the society I live in; never have I felt more poor and powerless— and this from an educated, middle-aged, middle-class, cis white male, a guy who has been dealt a pretty high hand in the game of "cultural capital." I don't understand or really trust law enforcement anymore, although I'll never be stopped just for Driving While White and I probably won't be shot at if I do something out of the way. I read my weekly *New Yorker* with increasing disgust at the lifestyles of the very rich and not even famous at whom the advertisements are directed; I toss out unread the glossy travel magazine to which something I have done entitles me to a free subscription, as the conspicuous consumption it ballyhoos makes me queasy and angry.

I'm not a liberal Puritan, at least by contemporary Massachusetts standards. I eat meat, sometimes even fast food, and I drive a four-wheel drive box that gets annoyingly poor mileage. We keep cats, and we sent our kids (at faculty discounts) to private schools. One of my kids was fourth-generation at a college now under fire for legacy admits, although there was no financial or other material advantage to admitting him, any more than there would have been for any of his schoolteacher forebears. I watch cable TV and buy the occasional lottery ticket. I am not a victim, nor do I choose to play that role, and I try to avoid sounding holier-than-thou, although I am self-righteous about bicyclists who don't obey traffic rules. I'm mostly a romantic optimist about things.

But today I feel lost. I don't know whether I live in a society characterized by its aspirations and opportunities or in a nation tired of aspiration and opportunity that is beginning to give in to all of its worst impulses: materialism, racism, apathy, selfishness, and a kind of pervasive sociopathic *schadenfreude* that allows us to observe myriad quotidian horrors and analyze them only for their entertainment value. I worry that we are becoming our own "daily beast."

Ferguson has only made my funk worse, but the election and the low voter turnout earlier this month were hard to bear. I can't figure out whether our national leadership in all three branches of government is cleverly playing some deep game or whether it is as adrift and broken as it seems. I trust that my economic future is at least moderately safe, but I won't be surprised if the whole shebang goes south one day. I'm not personally afraid of terrorists in my life, but part of me expects to be wrong on that.

It's very hard to be a romantic optimist on Thanksgiving 2014. It's hard to be grateful for my privileges when I know they come at a cost to so many others and when they actually seem to mean less and less against the extreme privilege of millionaires and billionaires. Things may not look as grim as they did when Abraham Lincoln called for a national day of Thanksgiving in 1863 in "the midst of a civil war of unequaled magnitude and severity" (as Lincoln put it), but they look a whole lot more dismal to me than they must have when the Plymouth colonists and their Wampanoag neighbors broke bread in the 1620s—the colonists happy that they had survived to start building their little theocracy and the Wampanoags happy for some more or less amicable (for the time being, anyhow) trade partners in their depopulated lands. Of course, that relationship eventually soured, affording me one more batch of unearned historical privileges at the expense of others.

Like a lot of us, I'm left feeling most grateful for my family and for the (I hope) benign privilege I have been given to seek happiness and sustenance in a field, education, that brings rewards well beyond the material. When our family of teachers and students gathers today to eat our ritual turkey, we'll have one another to be thankful for, and I can hope, as an educator with an obligation to be hopeful, that I can figure out how to transmute my current *weltschmerz* into humility and humble action and, indeed, *hope* for all of those of us who sit in discomfort with our privilege.

We just need to stop accepting the stratifications and inequities as "the way things are" and, especially for the privileged, to stop blaming the de-privileged and disenfranchised for wanting opportunity and justice. It shouldn't ever be, or appear, just plain absent.

Not Your Father's School, November 27, 2014

26 ANNALS OF TEACHING: BEING WRONG

The first members of the high school class of 2013 started walking across the stage weeks ago, and it'll probably be a couple more before they're all done. It's a time for celebration, a time for tears, for joy, for a few regrets, and for enormous pride. The grumps can claim that an American high school diploma isn't worth much, but try telling that to the kids and parents whose beaming pictures fill ten thousand Facebook pages.

It's also a time for teachers to take stock. That's our work walking across those stages, each flushed face a story and each diploma the merest token of lives together, theirs and ours. It's at least in part a story of our own hopes, our dismay, our sweat, and even our tears.

It's also, sometimes, a story of our mistakes. One of my little secrets (and I've occasionally found other teachers willing to acknowledge it as theirs, too) is the pleasure of having been wrong.

I learned about all this when I was growing up from my father, whose former students would often show up at the house, sometimes decades later, sometimes sporting a family and always sporting a story and a smile.

Pop would greet the visitors, sit them down, often them a drink, listen, ask a bunch of questions, and smile a lot. He loved these visits, these affirmations of his work—living proof that he'd done something worthwhile with his life, as if he weren't really quite certain; I'm not sure he was.

A theme of these visits was often, pretty clearly, the visitor's desire to do a bit of affirming on his own. A significant portion of them, it seemed, had left the school under something of a cloud; a few, indeed, had been expelled. There may have been hard feelings once, but no longer—never a sign of bitterness or anger. All was forgiven. As Pop might have explained it (but in fact he never tried), kids do stupid things sometimes, and sometimes those things have necessary consequences, but you need to be responding to the behavior, the decision, not to the kid.

I remember my first winter working at Pop's school, doing some substitute teaching and trying to set up a development office for a place that had never tried to raise a dime. One gray March day I was called to my father's office. He needed me to tend a student who had rifled the school secretary's desk and been caught. Now he was on his way home to Georgia, but his plane left later in the day.

Look after Talcott (not his real name), said Pop. *Why don't you drive him up to the sugarbush and show him how they make maple syrup?*

What? I thought to myself. Well, Talcott didn't have much to say that day, but he saw maple sap being boiled down and sugar hardening in molds. I bought him a little box of maple sugar candies to take home, and then we headed to the airport.

What was that all about? I asked my father that night. *Oh, he's not so bad*, was the reply, *and he's had a lousy time. I just wanted him to have something positive he might remember out of all this.*

I don't know whether Talcott ever came back to call, but he might have. My father would occasionally confess that some of his visitors were kids he hadn't had much hope for—so shallow or so incurious or so mean or so untrustworthy. Those visits were reminders that he'd been wrong, and the joy of seeing those characters redeemed, happy and successful, gave him real joy, as if the real redemption in each case were his.

And so I've grown comfortable being wrong. All the silliness I observe in kids, the behaviors that sometimes require intervention and occasionally generate my inner disapproval, is just part of their growing up, their time to make mistakes both excellent and idiotic, their time to try out new personas and new perspectives. Of course we sometimes cringe; making us cringe is practically part of their job.

Thus, commencement is a festival of memories, of impressions corrected. I sit and remember when I wondered what would become of them, when I despaired of some. It's astonishing, isn't it, what these kids have become, what they've accomplished and where they're going?

But there they are, proud and successful, high school graduates all. Every one of them is a story, and I realize that I don't even know, have maybe never really known, even the half of it, even if I might have had such-and-such a kid "all figured out" at some point. Their secrets and their dreams are theirs to keep, my worries and judgments mine to let go of.

Sometimes old students come back to see me, the old stars and the young reprobates, and like my father, I love them all. Sometimes they remind even me that I was wrong about them, and I'm grateful for the lesson, as happy as ever my father was.

There's nothing like being pleasantly surprised, now, is there?

"Independent Schools, Common Perspectives," *Education Week*, June 12, 2013

27   ANNALS OF TEACHING: ON NIGHTMARES

I have had a couple of conversations with teachers lately about nightmares—those anxiety dreams that many teachers seem to experience around the beginning of the school year. Underdressed, underequipped, and certainly underprepared, the dreamer finds himself or herself "on" in a situation, often but not always school-like, from which there is no escape and in which the often undefined audience can deliver summary judgment.

Several cycles of these anxiety dreams had passed through my consciousness before a chance comment by a colleague taught me that they are nearly universal among teachers, young and old. I found this quite reassuring, and now that we are in an era when sharing at least some of our worries is allowed, I've decided to treat my own pre-school nightmares as old friends who reappear on cue each August and whom I share with fellow teachers around the world. In time they drift off, perhaps enjoying an eleven-month vacation before returning to work. (Or perhaps it's not that long, as I suppose that the school year must be starting somewhere almost every day.)

For some teachers, however, the anxieties don't diminish, and the nightmares haunt their working days. I'm in correspondence now with a veteran teacher in their first year at a new school who is finding every day to be just such an experience. Feeling un-oriented, un-noticed, and un-appreciated, this teacher lives in a world in which every word feels as though it might be the thing that "gets me fired." The students have discovered that they can go to the teacher's supervisor and complain about the teacher's manner, standards, words, and even choice of materials, and that the supervisor's response—or lack of one—can unsettle the teacher. "Every day is hell," says the teacher. I suspect, from our conversations, that the teacher has retreated to a place in which instead of teaching each class, they are play-acting the role of teacher in the hope of getting the lines right to please the audience.

It's no way to live, and we have probably all been there: that period when something real or not quite so real seems to loom over our work to the point that we feel like Emily Dickinson's poetic persona stepping "from plank to plank, a slow and cautious way" and not knowing whether "the next would be [our] final inch." We're good people, and we're trying our hardest, but someone has questioned our work, fairly or unfairly, and dread fills the pits of our well-meaning stomachs and eats at our well-intentioned souls. In time something happens to reassure us, and we return to more optimistic attitudes and cheerier ways.

The living nightmare is probably a combination of things, at least some of which stem from schools' willingness to permit rumor or innuendo to linger when clarity and support would ameliorate matters quickly and effectively. The teacher may be spinning within their own unhealthy response to anxieties, but anxiety is a product of uncertainty: What are the norms and expectations of this institution's culture, and will I ultimately be supported and helped or just left to twist in the wind?

Three things, I think, would help my friend. The first would be a more focused and intentional indoctrination as to the ways and mores of the school; it's late, perhaps, but not too late, for a friendly mentor—a mentor whose belief in the both teacher and in teaching itself is strong—to help the teacher through this period with some thoughtful listening, advice, and affection.

The second would be evidence that the school is listening not just to the students but working to help the teacher and the students alike to bring their expectations into alignment. It's likely the teacher, lacking much in the way of aims and materials for the course they have been handed, has goofed, and students sometimes take our goofs as evidence of incompetence or even apathy. It is someone's job to sort this out, to redirect the teacher, and to assure the students that the teacher is working hard on their behalf.

The third lies with the teacher. After finding myself frozen with fear during the first couple of weeks at a new school many years ago, I was finally brought back by a loved one's sharp reminder to "Be yourself!" Like my friend, I had been trying to channel every teacher or teacher character I had ever known, no doubt becoming more inauthentic and more untethered in my work every day. It's a wonder my students—who had been gentle and supportive from the get-go—hadn't eaten me alive. In retrospect I hope they at least got some pleasure in imitating my "teacher voice."

So my friend, like all good teachers, must remember to remain true to the sources of strength and individuality in their character that have made them a great teacher and a great person. They need to dig deep for the sources of confidence and self that have worked for them for four decades already and to approach their students as trusted colleagues and their new faculty colleagues as friends and supports. They need to be themself, the person who is a teacher and not the person playing a teacher.

In time I hope their waking nightmares will end and that they will rejoin the rest of us in a world in which anxiety dreams come only at night as "nature's way" of annually reminding us to do our best—and to be ourselves.

Admirable Faculties, September 20, 2008

28 NARRATIVE COMMENTS, GRADES, AND SCHOOLS

For the past couple of months we've spent some faculty meeting time on the question of "comment forms." For those unfamiliar with this interesting little cultural wrinkle in American independent schools, "comments" (some schools say "reports," and there are probably other local usages with which I'm not familiar) are regularly scheduled narrative reports on student performance that usually accompany and sometimes contain term and year-end grades. Some schools write more of these, some fewer; sometimes they are lengthy and rich in content and observation, and sometimes they are more pro forma, even just pull-downs or pastes from a database.

At any rate, comments tend to be one of the things that set independent schools apart, a service that comes as a perk in return for a hefty tuition payment. Parents, we believe, expect them, and most of our schools go to a fair amount of trouble to make sure that a quality (i.e., well proofread and informative) product goes out the door.

The challenge, of course, is not just to be informative but to provide information that has meaning to parents and guardians and, for lagniappes, might even provide some useful feedback to students. Since most comment forms also include grades of some sort, there is a kind of imbalance between the perceived weight of the grade versus the weight of the narrative. Most parents and students focus first on the grade, then the comment—even placing the grade box at the bottom of the page won't prevent eagerly scanning eyes from spotting it before reading the accompanying text.

We'd like to do a better job. There are so many questions to be answered first, however, that our work seems to be on parallel tracks. One is the "get it done" track that just wants to have a new form "in the can," while the other, more philosophical track that wants to figure out not only what the audience for these things really wants, but also what we as a school should be *trying to say* with them.

Are comments supposed to be detailed reportage and analysis of a student's work—word by word, problem by problem—or disquisitions on intellectual character: curiosity, engagement, cooperation, enthusiasm, positive participation?

Ideally, I think they should be both, somehow balanced so as not to bury readers under excessive detail (and too often written in a school's idiosyncratic education-ese) nor snow them with too much character commentary. As a parent myself, I'd like to see comments that tell me how my child has been performing when faced with different sorts of challenges, and I'd also like—heck, I actually crave—some evidence that the teacher knows my child as well as his or her work. It would be great if this part were couched in the lofty goals to which we educators aspire for our students; I'm fortunate enough to work at a school whose mission statement includes terms like "reason and engage deeply," "be intellectually curious," "leadership and teamwork," "act effectively," "respect," and "compassion." How wonderful it would be to see these enshrined as required topics to be addressed in the written comments on my children's work that come home three times a year!

Lately I've been reading *Education Hell: Rhetoric vs. Reality* by Gerald Bracey, and in it he makes a fine case for the not-so-21st-century but oh-so-critical idea that schools must be above all about teaching students, not subjects. The book itself is about the overuse of test scores to judge education systems, but a logical extension of Bracey's argument is the overuse of grades to judge children. In the context of that reading our conversation about comments—and grades—has taken on a significance that I can't shake off.

The next stage, I suppose, would be a discussion of grades themselves: what their purpose is, how we generate them, how we use them. There is a great argument that can be made for doing away with them altogether, and some schools have done this successfully, but regrettably I'm not sure I see that happening at our place any time soon. But the comment discussion is a start, and even if the "get it done" concept prevails and we just rejigger our current form, we will have at least begun a conversation that I think will be hard not to continue as we get deeper into new and exciting work around curriculum and assessment.

Admirable Faculties, February 9, 2010

WANTING MORE FROM OUR WORK

Perspective by Thomas Mueller, *Assistant Head of School for Academics, Trinity School of Midland*

I have known Peter Gow for many years. I have seen him as a colleague, a mentor, a thought leader, a teacher, and in other roles. However, regardless of which role he is in, it is rare to have a conversation with him that doesn't quickly include the words "child", "student" or "change". In this set of blog posts, the word "change" outnumbers the others by a healthy margin. This appears to be the reverse of most of Peter's writings, whether books, blogs, articles or tweets.

In these readings he cuts to the chase and focuses on institutional obstacles to changes intended to improve the student experience. In typical Peter fashion, he highlights the unintentional processes that can lead otherwise dedicated educators to be the very thing that stands in the way of worthy initiatives. But Peter does not blame, he explains. And in explaining he shines a light on the path forward. In this case he has identified research showing how the best of intentions among school leaders can lead to less than desired outcomes. He shows how there are unspoken expectations for differing roles, such as supervisor, middle manager and academic leader. These roles have their attendant, and differing, skill sets. This itself can be at the core of much frustration. He also shows how this in turn can lead to some initiatives never attaining the influence they deserve.

So what can be done? Is it hiring? Training? School culture? Is it a management issue or a leadership issue? Read on!

29   MIDDLE MANAGEMENT—A NEW VISION

Arguably the one of the most interesting and compelling articles on leadership and management that I've encountered was "[What Makes Leaders Succeed](#)" in Korn/Ferry Briefings; alas, it's now only available as an executive summary. In its original full version, the article lays out the results of research into the effectiveness of certain kinds of managerial behaviors.

In a nutshell, the authors of the study (titled "Testing the Leadership Pipeline")—Robert B. Kaiser, S. Bartholomew Craig, Darren Overfield (all of Kaplan DeVries Inc.) and Preston Yarborough of the University of North Carolina at Greensboro)—have researched and identified the leadership skills and styles that are most likely to be effective for "executive," "middle management," and "supervisory" leaders. It turns out, in a latter-day echo of the Peter Principle, that the most effective behaviors at each level are quite different; the Korn/Ferry summary even has a nifty graphic to illustrate this that only my respect for copyright laws prevents me from inserting into this post.

In all the reading and work I have done on school change, I have been struck over the years by what I have come to call "The Department Heads Problem," the tendency of many school administrators to lay at the door of department chairs at least some of the responsibility for foot-dragging that slows and sometimes stalls change initiatives. The summary, and the graphic, started me wondering.

In our schools we often regard department chairs as "middle managers," and so I wondered how the positive traits identified by Kaiser et al. played out in my anecdotal experience; they didn't, quite. So I sent Robert Kaiser an email asking just how he and the authors of the study would define middle management, in schools and in business.

I was pleased when Kaiser responded not just with a quick answer—middle managers are "responsible for managing other managers...most functional heads are considered middle managers, too"—but also with a copy of the full study, which has kept me busy, and I have to say enthralled, for a day now.

By the definitions Kaiser et al. have drawn from the literature and set forth in the full study, "middle managers" in independent schools are NOT department chairs but rather virtually all members of what schools regard as their administrative teams or cabinets. The only real "executive" in most schools is the head of school, responsible to the board and the key player in enunciating and setting in motion implementation efforts for strategic plans. While a few schools may have associate heads or other "senior administrators" who may sometimes or even often function in an executive capacity, in most smaller schools even assistant heads are essentially middle managers, charged with oversight of either important school functions (finance and operations, admissions, development) or the leadership of academic divisions.

Department heads, in this schema, are "supervisors," not middle managers. Interestingly, the behavioral qualities associated with effectiveness at this level are "Learning Agility" and "Work-Life Balance." Predictably, "Abrasiveness" is highly correlated with non-effectiveness, but so is—get this—"Supportive Leadership." By the terms of "Testing the Leadership Pipeline," effective supervisors—department heads, mostly—are characterized by quickness of apprehension and the ability to compartmentalize work and personal life. Somewhat strangely, "Directive Leadership," "Empowering Leadership," and "Lack of Follow-Through" are neutral factors.

Schools are human places, where we put huge emphasis on such qualities as supportiveness and "empowering" others—these are the things we like to think we are best at. And yet, for the hundreds of supervisors in both for-profit and non-profit organizations studied by Kaiser and his team, these things don't much matter at what in schools is the analogous level, except insofar as supportiveness actually interferes with effectiveness. One imagines that many department heads, newly risen from the faculty ranks, might easily err on the side of being supportive of department members when a more matter-of-fact, nearly directive style is called for.

Empowering Leadership and (whew!) Abrasiveness are the negative factors for effective middle managers, but Supportive Leadership joins Directive Leadership and Learning Agility as positive factors; Lack of Follow-Through and Work-Life Balance are neutral. This made a whole lot of sense to me as I shifted my definition of middle manager upward to the administrators I have known and the work we are asked to do in schools. But being a directive leader can be a tough transition for a teacher-leader in whose world the gentle, supportive cajole is often the most effective tactic.

At the executive, or head of school level, Empowering Leadership—effective delegation—becomes a key skill, but Learning Agility is paramount, more important than for middle managers or supervisors. Directive Leadership (one thinks perhaps of micromanagement), Work-Life Balance, and (finally!) Lack of Follow-Through are strong negatives. Supportive Leadership and Abrasiveness are neutrals.

Much of the point of "Testing the Leadership Pipeline" is about the challenges leaders face when making transitions from level to level, and this later slide deck of a presentation based on the paper makes it easy to see what these might be.

For schools, in particular, the paper speaks to the importance of making careful choices when hiring or promoting, at every level. While the literature cited suggests a failure rate of about half of executive appointments, the failure levels at middle managerial and supervisory levels are not insignificant. How schools prepare staff for upward transitions is critical not just to the success of the individual but, of course, to the overall success of the institution.

I would strongly urge anyone involved with hiring and orienting department heads, school administrators, and heads to check out the summary and to seek out the finished paper if it still available. In it lies considerable wisdom, backed by extensive research, and a tremendous resource for independent school management as a whole. The premises and points could drive a whole new approach to recruiting and training school leaders.

I want to underscore that the point of the paper is not just about filtering or screening people, rejecting some and advancing others based only on personality traits. The big idea is that people can be helped to grow in known and necessary ways in order to be successful.

Admirable Faculties, February 2, 2010

30 A NEW ERA FOR DEPARTMENT HEADS—PART I

Wherever academic deans, division heads, assistant heads, and other academic administrators gather, one theme of private discussion is likely to be frustration with department heads. In what experience tells me is an unfair characterization born of the frustration of "designated change agents" in institutions undergoing some disruption as programs change, department chairs, it seems, are everywhere bodies of resistant, petty, disinterested so-called leaders who are in fact unwilling to lead. Furthermore, they are seemingly immune to anything like new ideas and lofty concepts of professionalism, even if they themselves are fine teachers and the ideas they are being asked to embrace self-evidently good for the school and its students. Why the resistance? Why the seemingly willful rejection of notions of professionalism?

What is troubling is that the answers to these questions are clear and comprehensible, and everyone knows them. Department heads in most schools are in fact being asked to do new work, under new conditions of accountability, with little or no formal training and even less recognition of all the dynamics at work in making their lives challenging. Work that was once securely in the hands of heads of school—who had taken on these challenges willingly and for appropriate rewards—has now devolved onto "academic administrators," who have in turn passed ever-larger chunks of this work off to department heads whose training and expertise as "managers" has come from—where?

For the most part risen teachers themselves, most academic administrators are depending on on-the-job training for their own growth as managers and supervisors; although there are increasing numbers of workshops and seminars where these people can gain expertise, the numbers suggest the primacy of OJT as the way in which most of such people scramble up the learning curve. While it is entirely logical and organizationally sound that they in turn should enlist department chairs to participate in carrying out the strategic work of the school—including teacher evaluation and curriculum initiatives—the situation becomes one of the fairly competent (even if brilliant and wise) asking the utterly unprepared to share their burdens. Often enough the administrators actually see this as a way of giving a vote of confidence to the department chairs, to enlist them in "big picture" work in a way that is sincerely intended to honor and even reward their expertise and experience.

Department heads in our time are perhaps not unjustified in feeling as though the rug has been pulled out from under them, just when administrators are sure that asking the chair to "step up" is the most sincere form of compliment. Instead, chairs, once occupying a sinecure that even tenured college professors might have envied, feel threatened and devalued just when their superiors believe they are offering changes in responsibility that will lead to an increased sense of competence, authority, and professionalism.

That this quandary seems to be nearly universal in independent schools ought to be a cause for alarm. The issue, I believe, demands serious attention as well as an honest analysis of the issues that underlie the problem. For some reason, we have not done a very good job of investigating the sources of the challenge, which seem simple and clear enough when one stops to think about them. And because of this, we have not always set about addressing them as intelligently and as effectively as we might.

The "solution" is complex, probably time consuming, and potentially expensive. In the end it involves serious training and in fact some serious examination of schools' fundamental personnel practices and the ways in which teachers are vetted and primed for leadership roles. It also involves an acknowledgment of the ways in which schools are and are not "businesses" and of the ways in which values must drive the work of educators.

But department heads can be redeemed as "middle managers" or supervisors and more significantly as real academic leaders. There are ways to bring chairs into common cause with administrators and to infuse their work with possibilities of satisfaction and professionalism of which they had not conceived. All of this work can make schools better and the experiences of their students richer, more meaningful, and more inspiring.

In a future post we will talk about the solution.

Admirable Faculties, December 11, 2008

31 A NEW ERA FOR DEPARTMENT HEADS—PART II

If lack of training and lack of engagement with or understanding of the mission are at the center of administrative frustration with department heads, it must also be acknowledged that classroom teachers report a range of their own frustrations with their middle management "leaders." Departments may or not be collegial environments, meetings may or may not be productive and enjoyable times, and the sense of direction and expectations may be unclear.

In the some unfortunate cases, unhappy or simply confused department leaders may look at the menu of tasks that have been laid upon their departments, measure the list against what they perceive as their own capacities or the "real" agenda of the school, and quietly pass along to department members permission to disregard any grand administrative directives—*Just do what you have been doing*, is the message; all this talk about curriculum or diversity or strategic direction is just window-dressing that we can safely ignore. In the worst case, the department becomes a kind of bastion against change, engaged in a passive-aggressive campaign against administrative initiatives it regards as fluff or even antithetical to the "real" standards and work of the department.

Solutions to these issues, whether they be just poor performance or active resistance, must address all of the problems that underlie them: the making of thoughtful appointments in the first place, lack of leadership skills, lack of understanding of the school's strategic directions, and a lack of meaningful authority (often exacerbated by the administration's actual withdrawal of support as the chair's performance lags).

This is, unfortunately, a comprehensively deficit-based model of department head development, with culpability shared by the school and the chairs. But it is important to set forth a caveat here that the underperforming department chair may actually have tremendous skill and administrative potential. It may even be that she or he is correct in questioning the school's commitment to the initiatives that have been passed down to his or her department. In this case the academic administration has its own soul-searching to do, a process that may need to move upstream to the level of head and board if the school is indeed guilty—as most schools are at some point—of enunciating grand principles and grand plans but then continuing business more or less as usual. (I believe the node of contact between principle and practice is currently to be found around a body of ideas and practice I call "The New Progressivism;" I blog about this HERE. This is another matter, for another set of entries.)

It is important also to note the difference between leadership and management. Leadership, in the context we are addressing, involves the ability to articulate a purpose and to engage others in working toward that purpose. As such, it usually but not always involves certain skills in management, which is the ability to organize and direct people toward a purpose; leadership requires a certain vision of which management perhaps requires less. It would be well for a department chair to be a leader—indeed, that is what schools claim to expect—but it is imperative that a department chair be at least competent as a manager.

In determining fitness for a department chair position, neither older seniority-based systems nor an enthusiasm to anoint a "young Turk" with creativity and energy guarantee ideal results. The qualities of an effective department leader are deep understanding of and passion for educational issues and the success of children, an ability to offer guidance to members on matters of both content and pedagogy, and some basic management skills (that can be learned). Along with these, however, must come a sophisticated comprehension of and positive engagement with the mission and core values of the school, and schools sometimes neglect to dig deeply into and then reflect on internal (and external) candidates' fitness in this critical area. Senior teachers may have retreated into their own sometimes skeptical or limited view of the school and its work, and less experienced enthusiasts, no matter how brilliant or energetic, may not fully comprehend the full significance or perhaps just the practical limitations of mission and values.

Leadership may or may not be a teachable quality, but there are certainly things that the school can do to invest in helping department chairs become viable and effective managers. There are innumerable professional development opportunities—workshops, multi-day programs, and even whole courses, face-to-face and on-line—with an excellent track record of helping participants learn how to set agendas, conduct meetings, deepen understanding of curriculum and instructional issues, perform meaningful observations, offer useful and professional-quality feedback to teachers, and provide mentorship to other teachers on issues of pedagogy, curriculum, and assessment. A partial list of great resources would have to include the publications and courses offered by Research for Better Teaching, the many workshops offered by ISM, and the Academic Leaders Retreats begun by the Independent Curriculum Group and now carried on by One Schoolhouse, which are less explicitly focused on skill-development than on helping participants learn to reflect on their work and set their own personal agendas for growth and efficacy. Regional independent schools associations, a few individual schools, and of course the Klingenstein Center at Teachers College are also great sources of leadership-development programs suitable for department chairs.

To engage department chairs in the higher-order work of the school, the first and most obvious step is to find ways to involve these people meaningfully in strategic planning and goal-setting. If school-wide initiatives have the aura of secret plans devised by what an old colleague of mine called "the high muckety-mucks," the psychic distance between the planners and those who must carry out the work will usually be sufficient to guarantee poor implementation. If the planners equally fail to understand the importance of communicating the value of the work to be done—whether in improved programming, increased efficiency, or even more effective branding and marketing—yet another failure factor is built in.

Thus, strategic thinking must first and foremost be an inclusive process and one whose products are fully and clearly promulgated to the entire school community in a manner that demonstrates the potential value of the work to be undertaken in strategic directions. Invite academic administrators as well as department heads into the process from the beginning, and not just into the actual development of the plan but into understanding the rationale for the planning itself and the long-term goals of both the planning and implementation processes; in other words, make a space to treat these "middle managers" and supervisors as leaders in order to help them internalize and take a stake in the school's loftiest purposes and aspirations. As with any effective planning process, the frame and touchstone for this work must be the mission and values of the school.

Proactive efforts to engage department chairs in serious work should not end with the publication of a strategic plan. They must be both consulted and included regularly and authentically in both the work of advancing the strategic directions and assessing and reflecting on all aspects of their work as leaders in curriculum and instruction. Rather than simply being given regular marching orders or asked into certain discussions as token presences, effective department chairs are given opportunities to speak to their work and the work of the school from positions of knowledge of and belief in the aims of this work. This becomes work that they relish doing, because it represents high-level collaboration; because it draws upon their best skills, ideas, and experience; and because they are acknowledged and appreciated for their professional and personal qualities. These qualities can also be enhanced by encouraging department chairs to participate in professional communities, whether as members of organizations like the Association for Supervision and Curriculum Development (ASCD) or by participating in discipline-related groups.

Chosen wisely, trained in essential skills, and included and invested in the high-level work of the school, department chairs at their best have no issues around their own authority because they possess both the competence and the confidence to move forward with their work as leaders and managers without the feelings of uncertainty or disengagement that are the root causes of the ineffective work referred to in the beginning of Part I (above) of this essay. They will be better guides and mentors for their teachers, cannier thinkers about curriculum and program, and more circumspect participants in discussions, formal and informal, of the school, its role, its challenges, and its future.

Admirable Faculties, December 22, 2008

TEACHING IN PERILOUS TIMES

Perspective by Rebecca Yacono, *Head of Middle School, Worcester Academy.*
Any educator who follows the tenets of Dewey, Sizer, or Montessori knows that what the school organizations and ed schools now call "21st-Century Education" has always been the purview of excellent teaching and robust learning. Through the lens of progressive education, so-called "21st-Century Education" is nothing new: hands-on inquiry, student-driven exploration, and authentic assessments are the very definition of learning. What *has* changed is the context in which those activities happen. The world has become increasingly complex and complicated, and fully understanding it surpasses everyone's capacity to inquire and explore. Over and over again, 21st-century educators are left only with more questions. In this series of posts, Peter Gow articulates many of the questions and thoughts on the minds of all of us who entered the field of education to leave the world better than we found it and who are discovering just what a daunting undertaking that is today.

32 *LOCKDOWN!*

I guess it's a part of life these days, but there is something chilling in reading over my school's newly adopted lockdown procedure: a reminder that much of what I have believed about the sanctity of the school and the schoolroom is headed the way of the slate tablet and slide rule.

School was always the safest place I knew. Partly, I suppose, this was because school was also literally my home. Upstairs for many years was a dormitory, and I have eaten enough dinners in school dining halls to make me an expert on chicken à la king and to give me a permanent aversion to tater tots; I find nothing ironically appealing about them.

But from elementary school forward, school was where I wanted to be, the place that provided my friends and fed my interests. Along the way there were enough locker room bullies, capricious or mean teachers, boring professors, and boorish schoolmates to teach me a few things about adversity, but on the whole, it was all a pretty good experience. I was reasonably successful at most of it (mandatory sports at my independent high school excepted), and I'm no doubt a prime example of someone good at school who decides to become a teacher on the strength of that experience.

I've had moments of vexation and even a bit of personal agony in nearly forty years as a teacher, but I've never felt unsafe. I've happily trusted in my adulthood and my experience to manage difficult situations and defuse a couple of near-fights among students. No guns, no knives, no threats—and certainly no maniacs or flying bullets. When I started at my current school in 1980, I got out of the habit of locking my car, and over the years this became something of a thing with me. The day I felt I had to lock up in our more-or-less suburban parking lot would be the day I started looking for a new job.

That day still hasn't come. I lucked out the day someone came through our school lot twenty years ago and yanked out a bunch of car stereos, though I suppose in general my vehicles haven't made very tempting targets. (*2020 note: Even in retirement, I never lock in a school parking lot as a matter of principle.*)

But now, like schools across the country, we get to learn what it's like to go into "lockdown." Where once our school doors were open and our building-and-grounds workers worried about leaky windows and keeping the baseball field in shape, now we keep most of our doors locked and depend on the crew to seal the rest should a threat manifest itself. We will teach our students where to go and how to act in perilous moments; it feels as though we are rehearsing the act of collectively cowering, however brave a face we may put on as we "shelter in place."

But cower we must. Maniacs and their guns are a part of our cultural landscape, and schools are no longer sanctuaries. As educators we all talk about wanting to give our students authentic, "real world" experiences, but surely we didn't ever mean this.

There's no lockdown procedure, however, for so many of the other things that can make school feel unsafe to a child. There is no lockdown from taunting and bullying, no lockdown from sexual exploitation, no lockdown from being misunderstood or having your learning needs ignored, no lockdown from workloads that drive students to depression and even suicide. For lots of kids there's no lockdown, either, from homes or neighborhoods where dangers, psychic and physical, pervade. And experience tells us that all these situations know no boundaries, that no private, charter, or public school can offer every child a perfect cocoon of safety.

Lockdowns are the uninvited guest, the evil witch, at the feast of "21st-century learning." Some of you, Gentle Readers, have known this for years, but for others of us it's a new thing: post-Parkland, post-Newtown, post-Virginia Tech, post-Columbine. Once upon a time priests and friars held out their arms to stop marauders at the church or monastery door in the name of god, praying that their consecrated spaces would be respected. Here we are, training to do the same, with no doubt many of the same prayers.

"Independent Schools, Common Perspectives," *Education Week*, April 10, 2013

33   SLOW-GRADING TEACHERS: CANARIES IN OUR COAL MINES

This is what students call "Early Decision week," and college counseling offices are quietly freaking out as they collate the last bits of paperwork to send off to colleges in support of students' applications.

When I directed such an office, the bane of my existence at this time of year were teachers who had left the writing of recommendations until the last minute. We had one egregious laggard, and it was often not until the afternoon of the actual due date that the letters would appear—sensitive and beautifully written, almost good enough to merit instant forgiveness for the stress that had been caused.

This same person had made life hard when I was academic dean, too, because they were (I'm trying to protect identity here) always horrendously behindhand in submitting grades and narrative comments. When they finally arrived, the comments were always excellent: thoughtful and reflecting a deep understanding of the students.

This teacher was also notoriously slow in grading and returning work, which was problematic throughout their tenure. I had occasion to poke and prod, as did the department head, the division head, and the assistant head of school. But the habits persisted.

In a couple of conversations—I was trying to be supportive—I made some progress, I thought, toward the bottom of the issue. Official deadlines for institutional paperwork are law for me, psychologically, but I, too, was a slow grader of essays and projects. I know all the arguments for speed in this process, and I buy most of them, but I know what hung me up sometimes and what almost paralyzed my slow-moving colleague.

Not to put too fine a point on it, the process of grading in traditional frameworks—A-B-C or 0–100 or 4.0—feels just awful to many of us. Even with the most prolific addition of comments, notes, and other kinds of feedback, the final act of adding a grade to a piece of student work, especially when the work must necessarily be evaluated with a degree of subjectivity, feels rather shy on justice. The grade feels like a judgment on the kid as well as the work, and many of us are wary of trying to judge the degree of real effort and thought that has gone into a piece of work. Sometimes it's easy to tell, but all too often it's not, and the grade, even in schools that have "effort grades" or other systems for stripping out the effort factor, is at best a crude approximation of something that is extremely difficult to apprehend.

Rubrics were my salvation, kind of. They at least provided a framework that helped me make broad-stroke evaluations of work and even tie those to something resembling meaningful standards for feedback. But they weren't perfect, and I was always aware that a few earnest students were writing as much to fit the rubric as they were to learn.

Many teachers find traditional grading distasteful, uncomfortable, and even personally wrong—the act of doing something that breeds cynicism and stands as a barrier between the work we are doing and the most sublime outcomes we could hope for. It makes us hypocrites when we measure ourselves against our ideals, and it makes many of our students into fearful creatures little better than Pavlov's dogs.

The slow graders, I think, are and have always been the canaries in our coal mines. They're telling us something by their struggles. Sure, some are challenged by time management and I suppose a few are just undermotivated, but their aversive response to the task of assigning traditional grades to each piece of student work is a message that these systems don't work well, that they don't really do what we want to pretend that they do.

Spend time with a group of deeply engaged educators, as I did last week at the Independent Curriculum Group's inaugural Academic Leaders Retreat. Ask them how much they like the grading system that they and their colleagues must use, that their students must experience. You'll not find many votes of approval for our current methods.

There are alternatives. Some schools don't give grades at all, and some have worked toward methods and language that describe student learning and provide excellent feedback without resorting to familiar numbers or letters. There are portfolios. Independent schools have missions and values that could guide them toward their own systems.

We blame the colleges for much of the standardization in the work we do; they'll expect to see the familiar, we tell ourselves. I hate to say it, but I think that schools ought thoughtfully and deliberately to test that proposition. After all, kids already get into college from schools that use alternative reporting systems and idiosyncratic transcripts. Maybe we need to find the courage of our deepest convictions here and see what we can do. Maybe we'll inspire a small hiring boom in college admission offices if it takes longer to read a file, and maybe we'll help inspire a whole new approach to that process—but that is for another day.

But I am happy to go on record as having enormous appreciation for my tardy colleague, as crazy as that tardiness may have driven me. I think I knew the depth of the anxiety that drove their aversion to a process that is, let's face it, pretty flawed on a good day and on others downright icky. That teacher was the canary in our mine shaft, and I think schools need to look for their own canaries and think about how to respond to the message they are sending.

Not Your Father's School, October 30, 2014

34 TOUGH TIMES: "PROFESSIONAL DEVELOPMENT AS R&D"

It's been a few too many days since last I posted here, and in the meantime the economic news in the fall of 2008 has gone from bad to worse to worse still; one presumes that sooner or later we'll hit rock bottom so that we can all begin to figure out how we will be living over the next few years.

One large probability is that independent schools will be hit hard by tough times. The *New York Times* is already writing about the effects on teenagers as families cut back, and for some families it seems likely that the tens of thousands of dollars they have been spending on independent schools will begin to look like an unaffordable luxury. We hope this doesn't happen–that the "valued added" of being taught by admirable faculties is compelling as a reason to stay put—but we would be naive to think that it might not.

In straitened circumstances, schools themselves are likely to be doing some cutting back. But I urge school administrations to take a lesson from the American automobile industry, itself now teetering once again on a brink that has become their position of choice since the 1970s.

American car manufacturers have consistently blown it when it comes to research and development—"R&D," the thing for which America has been most renowned, has been more about marketing for car companies than about improving the quality of their product. In the early 1970s Ford, GM, Chrysler, and AMC (remember them?) were committed to rapid model change with minimal technical improvement even as the rest of the world (= Japan and Europe) had begun to focus on quality, innovation, and economy. Nearly 40 years later, most American car models still lag behind their non-U.S. rivals in quality, reliability, and economy. Last week there was talk of GM and Ford looking at bankruptcy. Coincidence? Of course not.

For independent schools R&D is embedded largely in work each school does in two areas: curriculum development and professional development; the two are clearly interlinked. Great schools develop and keep great faculties by making certain that the best thinking and the most engaging, provocative ideas about curriculum and instruction are a part of the school's daily conversation. These schools go to great lengths to make sure that their faculties are deeply aware of how best practices can be applied in the classroom and how these best practices are evolving in the light of new understandings about teaching and learning.

The great advantage independent schools can have in this area is that they are mission driven, and as such they can be smart and thoughtful about how, when, and whether new practices are incorporated into their school's programs. The mandate schools have to figure out how to be better and then to become so comes not from state legislatures (except in the cases of a couple of states) or Federal agencies but from their understandings of their own purposes. Independent schools, in other words, have the privilege of determining the precise nature of the value they add to the educational experiences of their students.

Schools worried about enrollment or annual giving may feel the need to make some anticipatory cutbacks, but curriculum development and professional development are core activities that sustain the "value added" (and I admit to overusing this annoying term, which can smacks of education as a commodity rather than education as an experience) and more importantly the missions of their schools. Schools can only maintain program quality by keeping up the R&D that brings new ideas into classrooms and faculty rooms for mission-informed professional analysis, review, and implementation or rejection. In the great scale of things, the cost of professional memberships and publications and even specialized training for faculty is more than likely to be returned in the future if schools understand that these expenditures are investments to improve what they do and so sustain their position as attractive and worthy educational alternatives for families cautious about their spending.

"Professional development as R&D" ought to be schools' mantra as we enter an era of tough times.

Admirable Faculties, October 13, 2008

IN THE CLASSROOM

Perspective by Neal Keesee, *Associate Head of School, Christchurch School*

It is deeply symbolic—and important—that the first entry in this stimulating and inspiring collection of posts is a rumination on the age-old student question, "When Will I Ever Need This?" For Peter's impetus in this collection is to promote what is of lasting value for kids, whether that be progressive or traditional. Indeed, the key insight of this collection is to press us to ask again and again, "Why does it matter?" when we think about our practice as educators. And there is no better way to begin thinking about this question than to start with how the students we teach think and feel each day and to use that to assess our practices.

The writing in these posts is deeply rooted in the traditions of high quality Independent Education: taking our disciplines seriously, valuing the teaching of inquiry, and seeing real value for students in rigor. Thus Peter is not afraid to critique progressivism when it means lower standards. He writes about the importance of expository writing; about the place for content knowledge and memorization; about the real need for teachers to have deep knowledge both in order to inspire and to guide; about how design thinking and our use of failure in the classroom needs to acknowledge that sometimes failure does not lead not success but is simply failure with the lessons it brings; and about how technology is a tool, rather than an end in itself.

Ultimately, these entries are calling us to an authentic progressivism, to the embracing of best practices and good ideas for their goodness, whether new or old. They call us to a new progressivism that rings very true in 2020, when the promises of "Web 2.0" and other mantras of the last twenty years have turned out to be exciting but at times rather hollow.

That is not to say these entries are reactionary; they caution against the equally hollow mantras of test prep and the other tools of the educational-industrial complex that have led to something we all lament and which Peter mentions: by the time students reach high school they often have stopped asking why what they learn matters. They have to have their heads down to "succeed" and so no longer ask the question. There really isn't time to think with all the work they must do in order to get into college. There is passion here, a deep desire to give students the best, despite the pressures they face to perform.

And there are plenty of calls to look at various progressive practices—protocols and interesting ideas for snow days. Maybe when we miss school for weather, we should encourage students to experience that weather and write about it, rather than regret the lost assignment time. Indeed, a sentence that stands out in this collection is this, referring to the idea of building a snow fort: "Sometimes the doing of a thing is actually more important than receiving a grade, or even feedback, on it."

As an educator of twenty-some years, I believe that sentence is vital not only to understanding this collection but to what we do every day. Peter's collection is ultimately asking us to pursue our craft with nuance and balance, to be authentic and student-centered, but also rigorous in asking for the best from our students and from ourselves. Sorting out how to do that—anyone wrestling with competencies rather than grades will know this—is hard work. But it is work worth doing, and this collection encourages us to keep the faith, to keep our passion for teaching kids in the center of what we do.

35 "WHEN WILL I EVER NEED THIS?" FIGURING OUT HOW TO TEACH WHAT MATTERS

Back when I was a classroom teacher, the question I least liked hearing from my students was, "When will I ever need to know this?" My late spouse, who taught fifth grade, liked the query even less than I did.

We were lucky. She was teaching foundational skills in reading, writing, and mathematics, content that arguably shows up in most people's adult lives. Even if her kids didn't need to know the name of the builder of the steppe pyramid at Saqqara (part of her "Egypt unit"), they'll still see pyramids and maybe remember a few things (if not why the Lower Egypt is in the north and Upper in the south, but, hey.)

I was mostly a humanities teacher, and I came into the field when the old days of detailed grammar analysis and the memorization of lists of monarchs (with dates) were largely over. I could make the case for "critical analysis," global awareness, and effective writing, a case that might have been harder to make for being able properly to identify and use the past perfect subjunctive, or the rigorous diagramming of sentences (which I admit I sort of enjoyed as a student). At least when I periodically taught Latin, the whole enterprise was understood to be patently irrelevant in the sense of future application, except for "It'll help on your SATs." Did it? *Mihi vincet.*

I look back on this line of questioning and realize that I heard it less and less as I taught older students. "Why?" seemed ever to be on the tongues of my middle schoolers, but junior and seniors tended to absorb unquestioningly whatever they were being asked to learn.

It occurs to me that all learning in the latter years of high school, no matter how obscure or filled with tiny motes of content to be memorized, is probably seen, like Latin, as having enormous if utterly unfathomable instrumental value: "You need to know it for college!" And probably, too, for that awesome job you'll get after graduating from "a good college."

At the panel discussion that closed the Disrupting Education Symposium at Perkiomen School (an ICG Partner School in Pennsburg, PA) in November of 2018, the received truth of curriculum being relevant simply because it is what we have decided to teach came under fire from Ted Dintersmith (the producer of *Most Likely to Succeed* and the author of the recent *What School Could Be*) and others. I am guessing the other members of the audience were also a bit taken aback, for I imagine that just about every teacher finds themself sometimes hiding behind a kind of shield that protects us from looking at much of the content we teach from the point of view of whether we've ever used it in adult life. Factoring polynomials? I just figure math folks, CPAs, and scientists do it all the time. Splitting infinitives? I always imagine that someone in the Grammar Police is reading whatever I write, and so I try, usually, ~~to not~~ not to do it.

But factoring polynomials received unanimous acclaim from the panel for its notable absence from anyone's adult experience, as did Coulomb's Law—this from a panel that included two electrical engineers. No one dragged out "quantitative thinking" or "fundamental understanding" as justifications for having kids learn this stuff. Building "grit" through the process of mastery was about the best any of the panelists could come up with. (Or "up with which any of the panelists could come;" sorry, Grammar Cop.)

I've written elsewhere of relevance, but the points made at Perkiomen made me think about the concept in a new and clearer light. I don't want to start a debate with those who believe that all the minutiae of their course content is essential to a meaningful future life, but I wonder how much of what we teach in the belief that it is somehow paradigmatic could be completely—completely!—replaced by more practical, more authentically relevant learnings when embedded in far more experiential and problem-based kinds of curricula?

As I listened to the discussion at Perkiomen I was challenged to reflect on my own responses to "When will I ever need this?" I wonder now if my high-minded (and slightly defensive) belief in what I was doing clouded my ability really to see the implications of the question and to give an honest answer based on my own real experience. Maybe, or maybe not. But I finally realize that it's not a stupid or annoying question; at worst, it's just a slightly clunky adolescent paraphrase of the real question, "Why does this matter?"

At the risk of troubling your sleep, I invite you to ponder the totality of what you may be teaching and ask yourself, "Why does this matter?" There are solid answers, compelling answers, but let these answers lead you to deeper and more comprehensive ways of considering content.

As we seek these fundamental perspectives, I believe, we can begin to discern hints and even outlines of new and more effective ways of conceptualizing and teaching what truly matters.

Independent Curriculum Group Blog, December 9, 2018; originally in the ICG's December 2018 newsletter

36 TEACHING WRITING

I had a call from an old friend the other day who wanted me to write about the question, *Why can't kids write about history?* This teacher believes that students today have better and more sophisticated ideas about societies and the way they work and interact than the students she met earlier in her career, but she sees more and more of these bright, inquisitive, and creative students struggling to write well about history. *Where are the facts, the evidence*, she asks, *that support all these good ideas? Aren't schools teaching old-fashioned analytical and expository writing any more?*

These are great questions, and they are probably as old as formal education; one can imagine Roman tutors and medieval monks wringing their hands over their students' poor writing.

I suppose there are a couple of millennia worth of good answers, but I think part of my friend's concern is that her school, like so many others, has long embraced progressive principles. Unspoken in her question is a century-old critique of progressive education in general: the idea that somehow "progressive" writing instruction focuses on narrative or on the experience and opinions of the writer far more than it does on the construction of classically defined and structured argument.

For what it's worth, I really dislike this issue, in no small part because I think there is some truth to the critique; the last three or four decades have been very much about helping young writers to discover their "voices" and to reflect on and write about their own experience, to the detriment, in some quarters, of solid expository writing. In addition, the essays that were once familiar reading in schools as models of the expository form (think Bacon or even Montaigne, for example) have died the cultural death that has come, often appropriately, to so many dead white males. By the same token, thoughtful, tightly written non-fiction has drifted out of our schools as textbooks and test-prep have wedged their way in. An AP Biology student doesn't have time to read the reflections of Lewis Thomas, for example, en route to scoring a 5 on the examination.

I like to believe that the New Progressivism offers some help here, by reminding teachers that there is nothing un-progressive or anti-child about high standards. If good formal writing involves the generation of a strong thesis, the amassing of supporting evidence, and then the use of that evidence to build a connected, internally consistent argument, students need to learn how to do this.

It's actually countercultural, for those who like to think of themselves as that. Pay even the slightest attention to the current presidential campaign and see how the discourse has been reduced to sound bites, unsupported assertions, and statements of opinion. A couple of years ago Stephen Colbert and his writers created the word "truthiness" to describe the idea that something must be true merely because someone says and repeats it emphatically enough. In his little tome *On Bullshit*, philosopher Harry Frankfurt speaks to the unfortunate power of lies, including the Big Lie, to embed themselves in cultural consciousness enough to pass as truth, and of the increasing willingness of purveyors of ideas to depend on truthiness, or bullshit, to make their cases. I'm a big fan of Jon Stewart, but some nights I just want to deconstruct the program and derive and then lay out, with actual *evidence*, the points that *The Daily Show* makes and "proves" to its audience by implication, ironic reference, and even innuendo.

Therefore, it seems to me, there is something important and even urgent in teaching our students the classical structures of good expository writing and the paramount importance of supporting assertions not with more assertions but with actual facts. It's not hard to do this, although it may not be as much fun as assigning students the chance to probe their own psyches or to write deep short stories about dysfunctional families in the absence of sufficient critical feedback about the structure and use of evidence in these personal narratives.

New models of great expository writing abound, and the pages of the *New Yorker*, *The Atlantic*, *Seed*, *Slate*, *Orion*, and a host of other fine print and online magazines are filled with it every week or month. Go back a couple of decades to the best work of John McPhee or Annie Dillard or the more recent writing of Seymour Hersh for more examples; politics, culture, and the environment continue to inspire some of the best expository writing of our day.

Because I want students to be able to write compellingly and extremely well about history, and literature, and injustice in their own community, and the state of the environment. In part I want them to acquire this skill because it is satisfying, and because their college professors and future employers will appreciate it. I even want them to learn it because good writing reflects well on the schools and teachers—New Progressivist and otherwise—that foster its mastery.

Mostly, however, I want students to be able to write well because of the good ideas to which my friend referred. We are a world sorely in need of good ideas, but to prevail, these ideas will need to be presented with strength and substance. The Age of Truthiness must end someday soon, and then we will be desperate for alternatives that are authentic and above all, supported by the facts. Someone is going to have to save the world, and I think it's going to have to be people who think cleverly and who are able to convey their ideas as well as they think.

The New Progressive, October 24, 2008

37 MEMORY—IT'S A GOOD THING

Maryanne Wolf's *Proust and the Squid: The Story and Science of the Reading Brain* provides an amazing discussion of both the history and neuroscience of literacy. Wolf, a professor of neuroscience and child development at Tufts University, tells a compelling and sometimes moving story of how the human mind learned, as part of our social evolution, and learns, as children (usually) to read.

I found myself focusing on her analysis of Socrates' objections to the use of the written word, and it gave me pause to think about how as self-styled "progressives" in our culture we sometimes devalue the ability to remember, recite, and construct cogent, thorough arguments from the stuff of our memory rather than from data amassed as notes from texts. Sometimes the use of memory really is a good thing, and even New Progressivist educators need to acknowledge those places where memory, and memorization, can serve our students well.

Calculators, for example, are great things, but the automatic recall of basic math facts like multiplication tables, through the 10s, at least, is better. Anyone who has proctored a PSAT or other standardized test has groaned (silently, of course) at the sight of students using their TI-83 graphing wizard machines to do the simple multiplication steps of a problem; it's a waste of just about everything from battery power to time.

And technology proponents who glibly announce that students don't need to memorize simple facts (historical dates are frequently cited as the kinds of "useless" memorization that schools impose on their students) because they can always "look them up" fail to adequately acknowledge the role that deeply embedded facts play in giving structure to the rich contexts that we progressive educators try to help students construct. That the Declaration of Independence was signed in 1776, for example, doesn't mean much by itself, it is true, but it is essential in understanding the flow of the American Revolution toward alliance with France and ultimate victory. And why shouldn't students have some basic knowledge of momentous dates in their nation's history?

The 1776 datum is also useful in giving students an understanding that the Revolutionary War preceded the American Civil War, which came before World War I and the World War II. I fear I have discovered students in my own classroom who have struggled with this, and it's the kind of thing that "Polls Show Americans Know Nothing" news stories delight in exposing. Obviously, it's no longer necessary for chemistry students to memorize the periodic table or to have students master the monarchs of England in order, but some things are important to have learned by heart.

I'll risk sounding both pedantic and fussy (maybe even Dickensian, for all I know) by suggesting that educators ought to reconsider the wonders of human memory and how it can be effectively harnessed as a tool not just for superficial learning but as part of matrix of elements that go into teaching for deep understanding.

And check out *Proust and the Squid*—it's terrific!

The New Progressive, October 18, 2008

38 CONTENT IN THE 21ST CENTURY

While a part of a pretty interesting panel discussion on "The Future of Teaching" at the EdSocialMedia Summit at Beaver Country Day School the other day, I made the mistake of suggesting that teachers in the 21st century might need to be smart about content, along with other things like mind-brain-education science, child development, and curriculum and assessment design (along with technology tools, of course).

A fellow panelist was quick to take issue with that assertion, taking my meaning to have been that teachers would continue to be the fonts of all knowledge, lecturing their way back into the educational past.

Fortunately I had the chance to correct this notion, saying in my best Constructivist way that the necessary skill will be in knowing where the resources are and how to find them.

But I've been thinking about this, and I guess I'm going to stick with the essence of my original statement.

True learning, true mastery, is about nuance, about the dimensions of complexity and perspective that are part of deep understanding. I'd be hard-pressed to swallow an argument that master teachers need not be masters of the material they teach, darned near as excited by and engaged in their material as they are dedicated to the success of their students.

I hate to bring this up, since it doesn't gibe with many formulations of what 21st-century teaching should be, but a whole lot of successful people in many fields eagerly cite the teacher who inspired them.

The narratives tend to break down into two categories: the Teacher Who Believed in Me and the Teacher Whose Love of the Material Made Me Love It, Too. Teachers who communicate optimism and passion make a difference in their students' lives. In particular, the Teacher Whose Love of the Material Made Me Love It, Too is a master of content, able to share knowledge in an exciting and compelling way.

Then, too, do we think that primary grade reading teachers ought not be experts in their field? Or teachers in the STE(A)M fields, where our national anxieties focus on content knowledge deficits, real or imagined? Shouldn't even the mellowest "guide on the side" in a history class have a pretty subtle understanding of content in order to design and evaluate projects that bring students to deep and meaningful mastery of both the knowledge and concepts involved in topics like, say, the Civil Rights Movement, rivalries between Athens and Sparta, or the rise and fall of the Moghul Empire?

I had a flash as I was thinking about this that some of the most strident tech evangelists may have so internalized the notion that the medium is the message—a concept that works as we contemplate television drama or check our Facebook pages—that they have lost sight of the essence, the gravitas, and the grandeur of actual knowledge. Perhaps they believe that content knowledge is only memorizing facts, dreary and mechanistic mental drudgery of the most "industrial" sort. I bet, however, that they would be unhappy without their own expertise and a reason to share and apply it.

Some educators, I among them, are fond of Oliver Wendell Holmes's idea of "the simplicity on the other side of complexity"—which I take to be a kind of Zen-like deep understanding of difficult things that enables those who have it to see, and express, these things in a way that clarifies them for the rest of us. Those who have this capacity are the kinds of content experts that we are eager to listen to and learn from (and to hire, if we're being practical).

So let's not undervalue content knowledge. In good educators it has never been nor ever will be just about piling up facts and formulas; it's always been about using deep knowledge to pique, to provoke, and to inspire. All the social media in the world can't do this unless there are substantial skills, knowledge, understandings, and habits of mind to give the learning relevance, context, and authenticity.

Admirable Faculties, February 19, 2010

39   THE UNTAPPED POWER OF PROTOCOLS

I've been following the Twitter stream from the NAIS Science of Learning and 21st Century Schools Summit, and at this particular moment the magic word is "protocols." To my mind, that's deep magic, of the very best kind.

I first encountered protocols as a participant in Steve Seidel's Rounds at Project Zero back in the very early oughts. A parent who was also an educator told me, "Hey, you need to go to this," and I was hooked. At some point my kids' Saturday morning schedules began to get in the way, but I will never, ever forget my first experience at Rounds with Steve facilitating a Collaborative Assessment Conference Protocol; in one of the first couple of sessions the presenting teacher was an art teacher from central Massachusetts named Ron Berger, who brought samples of student painting and seemed to have some interesting thoughts on the work when it was time for the Presenting Teacher to respond to the group. Since then Ron has been something of a hero of mine, and it was awesome to be a peer with him last week at the [Transforming Teaching Design Convening](#) at Harvard, right upstairs from the place where Rounds is held.

I was so excited that I took the protocol concept back to my school. We found someone to train a couple of us, and we tried doing CAC Protocols as part of our professional development offerings, moving on to a Tuning Protocol or two. That summer we ran a faculty workshop and trained a bunch more of us to facilitate Looking At Student Work exercises; it was a heady time.

It didn't take long, however, for the bloom to come off the rose. As much as many of my colleagues appreciated and enjoyed protocol-driven Looking At Student Work, there was a significant group that could never quite warm to the process. As teachers, they felt—and defended their position—as though they were obligated to cut through the rigor of the protocol and get right to the business of problem-solving. Instead of seeing the protocols as a disciplined, structured, and rather egalitarian way to solicit input and drive deeper thinking on the things students and teachers might be working on, and sometimes grappling with, they saw the essential problem as the need to figure it out and start fixing things.

It's been twelve years since the very useful book *The Power of Protocols* (now in its third edition) first appeared, and the Looking At Student Work movement has been around since before then. (There is also the invaluable *A Facilitator's Book of Questions*, the product of several Project Zero mavens.) Critical Friends groups and other structured ways for educators to self-organize around issues in our practice aren't new. Why isn't protocol-driven work, in our classrooms and in our professional learning environments, more universal?

I believe the answer is that protocols don't seem to work well for some teachers. Whether it's because they are impatient, or they find the discipline dehumanizing (in the way that some teachers think rubrics drain the life blood from evaluating student work), or they just really can't wrap their heads around the concept as a whole, these folks feel an urgent need to slice through what they see as the clutter and get to sorting out the issue. (I suspect that this same issue is going to be getting in the way of our design-thinking-driven work for a while, as well.) We're teachers; we solve problems as expeditiously as possible in the moment—just as in the Geico ads, "It's what we do."

It may also be, and I suggest this knowing that it won't be a universally popular notion, that those of us who embrace protocols (and many of us who embrace design thinking, which in certain versions is a protocol in its own right) may be operating in something of an echo chamber—agreed as we are on the wonderfulness of our process, perhaps we aren't as open as we could be to the possibilities of those expedient solutions and the virtues of turning insight directly into action. I like to think that this isn't me, but then, we're all suspect narrators of our own consciousness.

Another reason may be that relatively few of us have ever sat through a well-facilitated protocol-based process; certainly my initiation at the hands of Steve Seidel, who models the passionate neutrality and deep wisdom required to make the most of the process with the skill of Yoda himself, was a special experience. But education is full of patient Jedi sages, and great facilitation can be learned. People may also not know of how many protocols there are, and how easy it is to tailor one to a specific need. (For example, I was particularly proud of the Comment Protocol at our school we developed for trying to coax insights about our teaching and curriculum from our term-end reports.)

There are likely to be many takeaways from the NAIS summit, and I hope that one of them will be to inspire more educators in more schools to explore the power of protocols as tools for thoughtful analysis of nearly every conceivable aspect of our work. (And buy the book if you don't believe me.)

Or at the very least, follow the Rounds at Project Zero site to see whether this wonderful experience comes back. If it does, next time you're in Boston on the first Saturday morning of a month during the academic year, stop by Longfellow Hall at Harvard and go to Rounds.

Not Your Father's School, May 19, 2015

40 FAILURE STUDIES

We've been reading quite a lot about failure lately, and clichés and nostrums aimed at getting teachers to embrace failure and to encourage students to do the same trip up and down my Twitter stream at the same rate similar exhortations to embrace "excellence" might have done twenty years ago, before a couple of stock market crashes (one just for dot-coms, one for everyone) and a brace of nasty, ceaseless wars. At least we're trying to be realistic.

Failure is pretty wonderful, we're told, and it is axiomatically the forebear of all success. It's certainly true that folks who don't experience failure, either because they're intentionally insulated from it by well-meaning but misguided responsible parties (parents and teachers and that sort) or because they are fortunate enough to get most things right most of the time, are in for a hard time of it when their ship inevitably grazes a rock or collides full-on with an iceberg. It is a truism that trial-and-error, the technique by which even the most intentional of us often wind up using to get from Point A to Point B, is very much about making and then correcting errors. It's an iterative process; so, pretty much, is everything. Welcome to the world.

Once upon a time I knew and loved a man who had devoted his life, quite unintentionally at first but ultimately with full awareness of his predicament, to failure. I'll not name him, but he was my father-in-law, a PhD neuropsychopharmacologist who had pursued his science after a stint as a medic in Patton's army, where he helped liberate, if that is the word, several death camps; he had come to the conclusion that the world was a pretty crazy place and needed all the help, scientific and otherwise, it could get. We'll call him Doc, which is how his neighbors, students, and colleagues referred to him.

By the 1950s Doc's life's purpose was clear: to track down the neurochemical roots of schizophrenia. In time he became a senior scientist at the Worcester Foundation for Experimental Biology, working next door to the team that created The Pill and changed society forever, although we can still work up a sweat fighting about who should be paying for a woman's right to choose conception or not—an important question in a nation where not every woman can easily pay for this herself.

So each weekday and sometimes more often for thirty years or more, Doc left the country home he and his wife had built with their own raised-on-the-farm hands and went to his lab. These were exciting years in neuropsychopharmacology, what with the emergence of all kinds of new tranquilizers, refinements of electroconvulsive therapy, and even some rather enthusiastic experimentation with psychoactives like lysergic acid. Doc even wound up doing some rather hush-hush work involving LSD, our government, and experimental subjects of various sorts.

By the middle of the 1970s, when I first met him, Doc had presented at the most prestigious conferences around the world, successfully applied for grant after grant, collaborated with some pretty serious players, and built himself a summer house on Buzzards Bay in Massachusetts—a modest A-frame where he and his family could relax, swim, sail, and stomp around in the mud at low tide for quahogs. Life was pretty okay, in general.

But some things were beginning to come into focus in Doc's field. It was beginning to look as though the particular theoretical route that he and his collaborators had taken into the mysteries of schizophrenia was, in fact, a dead end. The thing was, no one could be sure; more research was needed before the books could be closed on certain possible causes of this really, really awful disease.

So it was Doc's responsibility, his fate I guess, to chase these unpromising threads all the way to their cold, dead ends. Not surprisingly, the grantors were a good deal less excited about this work than they had been when success might have meant a cure, or at least a treatment. Now success meant failure, or maybe failure meant success, and the resources to do the work—and to sustain Doc's frugal, Depression-kid-who-remembered-the-bad-times lifestyle—gradually petered out; who wants to fund someone to prove that something indeed does not work? It was not a happy time in Doc's life, and so I never got to know him in his active, optimistic, Promethean prime, although his post-prime levels of energy and insight and know-how were intimidatingly high. He just never stopped being brilliant, and he never stopped being courageous enough to press onward with his work.

In time Doc retrained himself as a therapist and hit his "retirement" years with a new career and a chance to work one-on-one with people whom he'd once hoped to help wholesale. He died a few years back, the subject of awed tales told by his children, grandchildren, and acquaintances. I can still hear his voice, shouting over the chainsaw as we harvested the standing deadwood in his woodlot to heat his house.

But I think about our current love affair with failure, with its narrative of inevitable success after sufficient discomfort and iteration, and I am forcibly reminded that not everyone succeeds. In our society we've got plenty of evidence that failure often rewards even the most earnest and diligent effort, and

Doc's story reminds us that sometimes it's as critical to be sure that we're iterating all the way to the dumpster as it is to turn that sow's ear into a silk purse, or golden app.

In other words, failure in the narrative of "a stop on the road to success" is a lovely concept, but sometimes failure is just failure, and sometimes it's as important to end in failure as it is to succeed. But it's not always so fun for those who must endure, and sometimes even engineer for themselves, such failures.

As educators we sometimes need to check our tendency toward giddiness when it comes to counterintuitive but self-evident narratives that seem all new and exciting. I'm all for trial-and-error, failure, prototyping-and-iteration, but we need to keep our delight in these things in context and perhaps set ourselves and our students to considering other dimensions of failure. Whether we're talking science or social justice, there's plenty to explore and plenty to learn, lessons as important as failure itself.

Not Your Father's School, July 10, 2014

41 TECHNOLOGY, AND THEN SOME

I've been trying to update the look and functionality of my blogs over and above the cosmic wisdom of the posts themselves, and I find myself focusing quite a lot on technology. The links, widgets, and feeds that form the corona around the intended content are almost blinding, but I think that we're not going to be living without their like again. It's really too early to know what Web 2.0 will really bring, but already the possibilities seem endless, and even some of the old technoskeptics in my world are beginning to succumb. Give a man a phone, and he can make a phone call; give a man an iPhone, and he dreams he can do anything. (And yes, I have one, an "old" one, and I envy the 3G crowd and am shamelessly plotting to leapfrog them when the next iteration arrives; I check *MacRumors* every day in hope....)

But one of the cool things about the New Progressivism is the understanding that technology is a tool, and not an end in itself. If the tools of 2.0 seem compelling, it is because they support goals of collaboration, advocacy, self-expression, and creativity that are the hallmarks of the movement, and teachers quickly learn that students fluent in their use can move quickly to a mastery of skills and content and to depths of understanding that would simply not have been so attainable in a world without digital media. The possibilities for acquiring and using better and more complex data and for creating, editing, and polishing presentations in all media are simply astounding, and the best students become expert at technologically facilitated learning that is profound, real, and lasting.

The trick, of course, is to learn how to process and evaluate what students can do and are doing in ways that align with high, explicit standards and lofty, clear values. We have all seen student work whose form glitters with its own corona of bells, whistles, animations, widgets, sound files, and sheer cleverness but whose substance falls far short of demonstrating the intended learning. Teachers creating rubrics for the 2.0 world need to be astute, not astounded, when confronted with such work, and we need to be able to guide students toward truly effective and sustainable learning using technology. To this end, teachers will need to understand how it all works, even if they are neither expert in application nor wedded to the world of 2.0 in their own lives.

Thus, technology, and in particular the technologies of Web 2.0 and the world to come, may seem to be taking a place of primacy in New Progressivist thought, and I think this is all right for now. We have needed to accelerate rapidly in expanding our skills as educators in order to integrate new thinking in cognitive theory, curriculum design, sustainable development, and multicultural education into our work, and we now have a compelling body of possibility from the tech side. Our students may be digital natives, but it is our job to harness and hone their skills as substantial tools in our common struggle to teach and learn in the name of global equity, opportunity, and security.

A goal of New Progressivism is to create "all-terrain" students, able to function and thrive in any cultural or intellectual milieu. Our students intuit that cyberspace is not a void that separates us but rather a membrane that connects us, but as educators we need to believe and act on our belief that there is even more: that connection is only the beginning of common effort and collaborative enterprise with the very highest of human purposes.

The New Progressive, September 20, 2008

42 SNOW DAY THOUGHTS FOR EDUCATORS– AND PARENTS, TOO

The phone rang at 5:22 this morning, and she would have slept through it. But I answered and handed it to my spouse so that she might receive the news that she could go back to sleep. Her school was closed.

This has been a common scenario this year all over the country. Extreme cold, wind storms, snow, ice—the weather has been closing a lot of schools. And all over the country, educators are struggling with the obvious implication of all this, which is that students don't learn much when they're sleeping in or planted in front of glowing screens instead of being in school. What to do?

Some schools, presumably those with pretty well developed cultures and capacities in the areas of online and blended instruction, simply "flip" their programs and ask students to wire up for Google Hang-outs or Skype chats or asynchronous instruction. It's like school, only at home. It's a stop-gap, but it allows teaching and learning to go forward in ways that at least allow the schools not to feel remiss.

A friend's children attend an independent school in Atlanta (Mount Vernon, in the interest of full disclosure), where they are exploring nature's extremes in depth this winter (although my Buffalo upbringing makes me secretly scoff at their idea of depth), and their school has a kind of sensible approach to the snow-day problem. Teachers post work assignments on line by the normal start of the school day, and kids check in a couple of times later on.

My friend's kids are in mostly self-contained elementary classrooms, and I was really excited to learn that one child's daily assignment was, "Build a snow fort, sit in it for a while, and write about the experience." (LATER CLARIFICATION: The assignment was simply to build a fort; it turned out there was not enough snow, so my friend's daughter built her fort of blankets and bedroom furniture.)

I know you couldn't do that in Minnesota this year, what with those sub-Arctic windchills, but I just kind of loved this assignment: embrace the exciting thing that's happening, experience it, make something, and then reflect on the experience—just what I think I'd have wanted my kids to be doing back when they were home for snow days. (One of ours learned to cross-country ski on a snow day; to date he has only ever skied on snow-covered streets and campus pathways.)

There's an analogy here to summer reading, I think. It's all about time out of school, and learning. If you, Gentle Reader, happen to work in a school and were to send me a nickel for every minute you and your school have spent over the years discussing summer reading and the dreaded Accountability Question, I could comfortably retire. Snow days generate the same issue. I listened yesterday to a radio interview with a school official somewhere who outlined his district's great plans and snow-day assignments only to hear him mumble toward the end that the kids would actually have a few weeks to get the assignments done.

I offer up this idea to schools hung up on snow days and the Accountability Question. Instead of focusing on driving through The Curriculum, why not come up with a menu of developmentally appropriate general assignments that focus a bit of intellectual or creative exploration and some reflection? I'd even just go with one assignment per grade level; after all, the kids still have the discipline-specific homework they had for the snow day.

How about asking seventh graders to think and write about a hobby they wish they had time to take up, and why? What's exciting about it? Or asking tenth graders to write a little op-ed on a current events issue, or something relating to healthy or safe living specific relating to teenagers? If your school is quick with technology, you could ask kids to tweet or blog their responses (hey, Tumblr is made for this kind of thing). Ask sixth-graders or seniors to write three haiku on their thoughts and feelings on the day. Make a piece of sculpture from things you find around the house—or a snow sculpture that you photograph. If you must have accountability and an audience, this is what advisors are made for—they don't have to grade anything, just look, check off, and respond or give feedback if they wish.

(OK, I understand that this idea won't serve if you're in a school or district where state testing drives everything; every moment out of the classroom in some places, whether for snow days or recess, puts school and teacher performance—and even retention, god help them—at stake. Until more sensible minds are running the show, I get your need to keep hammering away at test prep. If your school lives and dies by AP scores, and if you really believe it does, I guess you're stuck, too. I would acknowledge, too, that many children do not live in connected households, and some assume other home and family obligations on accidental "holidays;" schools can only expect what they can expect.)

Sometimes the doing of a thing is actually more important than receiving a grade, or even feedback, on it. Instead of turning the dining room table into a mini-classroom for the day (it's already worn out from doing duty as such every evening), turn the house, the community, the world into a resource or a place of exploration; turn being snow-bound into an opportunity.

John Greenleaf Whittier's long poem *Snow-bound* is an enduring work of art that is also perhaps an overly loquacious meditation on memory. Why not come up with a handful of snow-day "assignments" that give kids an opportunity to think about and perhaps even remember something as new and fresh as the white stuff falling from the sky?

The Interested Child, February 13, 2014

THE CULTURE OF TEACHING

Perspective by Jonathan Martin, *Educator, Educational Writer, and Consultant*

Peter Gow is a teacher's teacher and a student's student. In many an ICG/OS retreat, Peter quickly took up the identity of "Uncle Peter," dispensing stories of teaching in the seventies, the headmasters he has reported to, the pretzels he had to make of himself providing what we now call "deeper learning" in school cultures that prized their place in the Ivy League rat-race. He's the author of, after all, the defining book about the profession of independent school instruction. At the same time, however, he's among the most enthusiastic learners any of us will ever encounter among our fellow experienced educators.

Peter is a Janus, looking backwards and forwards in equal amounts. A faculty "brat" who grew up on independent school campuses in the fifties and sixties, very much aware of his family's long schooling history, Peter regularly draws upon decades and decades of educational traditions, customs, and norms and distills them into an accumulated wisdom of good practice. At the same time, as all who know him know, Peter has deeply embraced and immersed himself in a myriad of projects both to forecast and create "schools of the future." He's written widely on the topic for NAIS; he's helped to invent the Beyond AP movement nationally; he's contributed to online school innovation in association with a slew of these initiatives including of course One Schoolhouse; and he's been "present at the creation" of Mastery Transcript Consortium and other critically important efforts to reinvent schools. His essay here on "Teachers and Change II" (the best of the bunch, not to be missed), showcases his reconciliation of preserving traditional schooling virtues while welcoming disruptive change and new paradigms.

Peter easily empathizes with and effectively articulates both the teacher's and the administrator's viewpoint. Many of us, myself surely included, have distanced ourselves, not by intent but in actuality, from our "teacher hat"—that worldview and sensibility—after becoming administrators, and despite our sincere professions have not genuinely continued to truly "own" that perspective. But Peter has, and he makes it clear in every conversation and every essay, even after years and years after he left full time instruction.

Finally, the same Peter who sees so much opportunity in snazzy technology and finds virtue in Clayton Christensen's writings, is the ultimate humanist among us. Read him write of "family meals" in junior boarding schools, or of the power of banter to level hierarchies and strengthen community in every context.

We've been so fortunate to have had in our midst Peter Gow—the Hegelian synthesis of all that we prize in schooling, the writer, the correspondent, the conversationalist.

43   TREATING TEACHERS LIKE GROWN-UPS

It'll take me a while to collect all my thoughts on the "Leading Toward A Sustainable Future" workshop this afternoon at the NAIS 2010 Annual Conference. I led off with some collective wisdom on school leadership that I had amassed for an online advisory for NAIS titled "Alive and Well" (about schools that were thriving through the Great Recession), then NAIS president Pat Bassett spoke in detail on financial modeling and how schools need to prepare to face "The New Normal" of limited resources. The interactive part for the good-sized audience (about 63 for a session originally planned for 40) was a panel presentation featuring school heads Vance Wilson of St. Albans (DC), Merry Sorrells of St. Paul's Episcopal School (LA), and Katherine Dinh of Prospect Sierra (CA). Paul Miller of NAIS moderated, and I filled a seat at the far end.

I was gratified that one of the themes I had identified, "Treat adults—especially faculty—like grown-ups," surfaced several times in the panel discussion. The point is that schools need to trust that adults in the community, and in particular teachers, are able to "handle" complex and complete information about finances. Katherine Dinh referred to addressing "the elephant in the room"—possible layoffs or salary reductions—when discussing possible ramifications of the economic downturn with her faculty (but it all turned out fine), and Wilson and Sorrells urged those in attendance—mostly school heads—to do the same.

It used to be considered axiomatic that independent school teachers would either be frightened by or simply wouldn't be able to grasp finances, and so the benevolent paternalists of olden times kept these sordid and baffling details from teachers. Thus, a teacher might not know until the last moment that his or her job was at risk, or—worse—rumors took the place of real information. Anyone who thinks teachers don't think about or understand money is badly misinformed, and on any faculty the combination of financial uncertainty and administrative secrecy about money matters is a powerful cocktail, toxic to morale and efficacy like almost no other.

I like to believe that the days of such "benevolence" have long passed, but that may not be true. But there is enough economic uncertainty in the world at large to make it more important than ever for schools to make a point of sharing financial information—including uncertainty—with their faculties and staffs.

There was plenty more to think about in today's session, but it's nice to think that leadership for a sustainable future now officially includes treating teachers as if they might be capable of understanding the financial contexts in which their schools operate. It's just too bad that this message still needs sending.

Admirable Faculties, February 24, 2010

44   TEACHERS AND CHANGE—PART I

Wherever people who see themselves as innovators or who are indeed designated agents of change gather, there's always talk of how resistant teachers are to change. Whether they are tech people charged with bringing a school full of teachers into the next, or rather the current, millennium, or whether they are administrators filled with the zeal of curriculum or assessment reform, the chatter—some of it not very sympathetic—is about how teachers' reluctance to incorporate new ideas and new ways into their practice is "hurting kids." Why, the question is asked, can't teachers see that the new way will be better, and that in the end it might even make their lives easier?

I spent fifteen years as a teacher-leader and then an administrator working to promote fundamental change in our own faculty, and in my work with other schools change of some sort is almost always at least a subtext of what I might have to say about professional culture or curriculum. I can say with embarrassed assurance that I too have shaken my head and probably banged my fist over the apparent conservatism of my peers as they dragged their feet in implementing great ideas that would indeed have served kids better, improved teaching, and in the end even made their work just a tiny bit easier. I'm not proud of all my past behavior in that regard, and over the years I have tried to think long and hard about change in schools.

Let us be clear: I like change, but what I am trying to do here is to think out loud about why so many teachers seem not to. The sad part is that this conversation echoes what so many people in American society at large seem to think about teachers in general: that they, particularly the ones in public schools, are a vast monolith, nice enough in their way as individuals but collectively committed by their politically powerful unions to an hysterical defense of the status quo. Not only do these people have their summers off, but they also refuse to make important changes—i.e., to revert to the ancient practices and rigorous standards that would instantly make our schools what they were 60 years ago. Whichever the type of change teachers are reluctant to make, they're seen as wrong: reject traditional ideas, bad; reject progressive ideas, equally bad.

The careful reader will have noted in the second paragraph above the lethal phrase "great ideas," and therein lies the rub. By the time the average teacher enters the second decade of a career, he or she will have heard or read about so many great ideas about teaching, learning, and curriculum that his or her head ought to be spinning madly. Much has been written about educational research or its lack, but the sum total of all the breakthrough ideas in education in the past twenty or thirty years, plotted on a continuum of "this way is better than that way" might amount to a zero-sum. For every new idea about pedagogy that demonstrates that student-centered teaching is better, along comes a study of the KIPP schools that proves the absolute superiority of direct instruction. My mailbox fills up each month with printed magazines that tout the value of computer-based instruction, but I can read dozens of blogs whose theme is worry that printed text is dead and that children are becoming stupider by the day in a digitally driven world. Whole language, or phonics? Math wars, anyone?

While the scholars, gurus, and school administrators with enough time and need to "keep up with the profession" consume their journals and blogs, classroom teachers barely have time to teach their classes, evaluate their students' work, and plan their next set of assignments. Where these tasks are no longer done in isolation for an audience of the teacher and his or her students only, there is the added anxiety of doing in semi-public what teachers long did in private: on-line gradebooks, assignments, and class notes add elements of external review to these aspects of practice, and the slowly evolving trend toward more professional conversations in school forces a new level of intentionality upon teachers' work. For many teachers, even these seemingly innocuous structural changes are difficult enough. Toss in the long-overdue movement toward consistent and thorough teacher evaluation, and it's not too hard to see why those elements of change in the landscape of teaching dismay many teachers when even more "great ideas" appear on the agenda. They know they will be held accountable in the end, but in the beginning they are scarcely able to see what it is that they are supposed to do, much less understand how to do it well. As one frantic teacher once said to me in a meeting, "What's the expectation? What's the expectation?" My expectation was that whatever the great idea was, it would make her work ever so much more simple; getting there would be the easy part. She, on the other hand, wanted to know where "there" was. In retrospect it was highly unfair of me to assume for others that we would know our destination when we saw it just because I was certain that I would.

The educational consultant Jacqueline Smethurst once cautioned the administrators at our school against falling victim to the "tyranny of good ideas"—being seduced by so many of the wonderful ideas that would emerge as we entered a process of curriculum review and development that we would soon be distracted from our main path. Wise leaders will consider this, but experienced teachers understand it instinctively, as it represents what they fear most about institutional change: a headlong, higgledy-piggledy rush toward not one clear goal but a number of obscure ones. At best, the purposes of the work become confused. At worst, all goals are forgotten, with only the unsettling memory of the "initiative" remaining; things might change, but to apparently little purpose and in unintended and perhaps even unrecognized ways. Initiatives that have blossomed and then died on the vine are the sources of much cynicism and inertia among teachers today.

(In Part II we will look at how schools might effectively manage change and mitigate its deleterious effects on the morale and efficacy of teachers.)

Admirable Faculties, November 22, 2008

45 TEACHERS AND CHANGE—PART II

In the previous post I suggested that a part of teachers' notorious reluctance to embrace change in their schools and in their practice comes from having experienced a surfeit of "new ideas" and initiatives that have meant a great deal of professional sound and fury—workshops, seminars, committees, planning sessions, new lingo, new gadgets—but that have in the end signified little in terms of real, substantive school change. There has been a whole lot of stress, in other words, but often very little to show for it.

Not to contradict myself, but I think that in many ways this explanation is too easy, even a cop-out. "We tried this back in 1985, and it didn't work," or "We heard this all before when they told us that [name the practice or idea] was going to change everything, but we're still pretty much doing the same old thing; somehow it just disappeared, or the administration just forgot about it" are too glib, too simple. Sadly, excuses of this nature allow teachers to sell themselves short by positioning themselves as passive-aggressive warriors(!) standing firm against the ill-considered whims of administrators and educational thinkers. At its worst, it's a pathetic stance.

The other day a teacher returning from an exciting presentation by one of the foremost gurus of our time complained to me, "Why don't the administrators ever talk about this stuff when it's over?" It is a fair question, and one that demands an answer if we are to understand the relationship between teachers and change clearly.

Like teachers (which many of them once were), administrators are besieged by good ideas; because their work often requires delving into professional literature and discourse, administrators are probably exposed to even more of them. They, too, have memories of guaranteed paradigm shifts that never happened and of painful, fizzled experiments in their classrooms and their schools.

To bring a powerful new idea back into a school and to sustain discussion of it presupposes the presence of a number of relatively unlikely circumstances. One is that a critical mass of people within the school know about and understand the concept to start with. The second is that there exists the likelihood that a groundswell of interest and support will keep the concept moving forward. And finally, the idea, whatever it is, must be consonant with well-understood and agreed-upon ideas of the school's own mission and values; it is especially important that the school's governing body be conceived of as seeing an organic, natural relationship between the new idea and the ideals and identity of the school.

Another friend suggested to me this week that in the past four decades there have only been a handful of true paradigm shifts with the momentum to engage (and to frighten, it must be acknowledged) all independent school educators. The first of these is the movement that can be described in most general terms as being about diversity and multiculturalism. The second relates to the whole matter of learning styles and learning differences. The third, just emerging but potentially the grand-daddy of them all, is the impact of technology, in particular "Web 2.0" in all its manifestations, on the way we think about curriculum and the role of schools.

Multicultural education and increasingly diverse educational settings have demanded that an overwhelmingly white population of independent school teachers to think in new ways not just about daily practice and relationships with students but about themselves, and about their role in a society characterized by a history of racism and the granting of unearned privilege to people in certain categories. The challenge of the work for many teachers has been to keep their own understanding evolving as theory becomes more sophisticated in an endless but necessary course of soul-searching and self-education. Those of us who were told in the 70s that "color-blindness" was the key have had to learn that acknowledging and understanding difference is truly the path toward understanding and efficacy, for example, and that becoming that "all-terrain" teacher is hard work with no end. As even the most conservative of schools took on the challenges of becoming more inclusive and diverse, teachers could not in the end resist this change.

In some schools there has never been an aversion to acknowledging that students' minds come in many flavors, but in many established independent schools teachers have struggled with the notion that some students might learn differently not because they are lazy or stupid but rather because they are wired differently. When issues of learning style or accommodation were first raised in such schools, there was often a sense of disappointment or failure—that somehow that school's "greatness," as reflected in the intellectual quality of its students as measured by traditional standards such as college or next-school lists and standardized test scores, was threatened, or lost. Teachers were often quick to blame the administration or the admission office for "lowering standards," for admitting students whose need for extended-time testing or extra help was a sure sign of their deficiency and the admission office's lazy willingness to "accept anyone" in return for suspect pay-offs—in athletic skill, perhaps, or development potential. It has been hard work for leaders in schools undergoing this transformation—or rather, doing the hard but necessary work of understanding the nature of intelligence and the complex business of learning and thinking—to give faculty first the understanding and then the tools for working in "cognitively diverse" classrooms. Of course, classrooms have been cognitively diverse all along, but what was missing was schools' and teachers' commitment to learning how to help ALL students succeed and not being satisfied that a bell-curve grade distribution represented a kind of natural educational morality.

The latest disruption in teachers' working lives seems to be coming from the role that new technologies can play in teaching and learning. The educational blogosphere is abuzz with commentary, for example, on the brilliant and controversial insights of Clayton Christensen and company in their 2008 book *Disrupting Class: How Disruptive Innovation Will Change the Way the World Learns*. Within a very few years, Christensen and his fellow authors say, schools will have moved to learning models in which curriculum and instruction is drawn largely from highly customized online sources. Schools will be very different places, and the role of teachers will be very different, too. Teachers will have to embrace the new paradigm, and there will no longer be places for those who do not or cannot do so.

(I might add that upon first reading, I loved what *Disrupting Class* has to say, as in many ways its thesis and content support the "New Progressivism" ideology that I have espoused for some time, and it suggests how the equally disruptive ideas of Daniel Pink's *A Whole New Mind* can become not just aspects of but the basis for real educational practice. But I digress.)

Here are changes that teachers have largely been unable to ignore or resist, regardless of the nature of the schools in which they might work. When it comes to changes that matter, and that truly benefit students, even the most jaded teachers are likely to come around in time; if they don't or can't, they leave the profession one way or another. I'm not so naive as not to know that readers are thinking of a teacher or two in their own schools who are still unreconstructed on these matters, but for the most part the resisters have either gone or have so marginalized themselves within schools (who should be finding ways to either help or remove them) as to be functionally invisible.

The answer to the original question, *Why are teachers so reluctant to change?* seems relatively simple, but the power of simple answers is always in their essence. Teachers can and will change when the new ideas and ways they are being asked to embrace are absolutely and fundamentally connected with serving their students in ways that are profoundly better. Change is no harder and no easier for teachers as a group than for any other slice of humanity, which history shows us has been extraordinarily slow to give up such things as slavery, sexism, racism, capital punishment, and war.

The challenge for administrators, educational thinkers, and other would-be agents or cheerleaders of change is to connect the "new" approach, whatever it might be, with fundamental values and fundamental value, and then to work like crazy to see that the message is never lost and that the training, reflection, and professional conversations through which teachers process change in their professions (as we all process change in our personal lives by sustained conversation and reflection) never end and are never diverted from the primary purpose of helping teachers accomplish hard things—hard things, yes, but great things!

In the end, ineffective ideas and clearly outmoded ways cannot resist good ideas. Even the best of those "great ideas" that I once pushed so hard but saw being ignored wound up taking root, not because or in the ways that I espoused them, but rather in better ways, mediated by the daily work and earnest reflection of teachers themselves.

What we cannot forget is that teachers tend to be born optimists who believe in children far more deeply than they believe in schools or educational ideologies. When ideas come along that are good for those children, teachers will, in time, accept, embrace, and then incorporate those ideas, not to please enthusiastic administrators but to serve their students.

Admirable Faculties, November 30, 2008

46 BANTER AND SCHOOL CULTURE

A friend, knowing I'm an old maritime fiction (Patrick O'Brian, Richard Woodman, and Alexander Fullerton are among my favorite authors) as well as an admirer for the leadership of Captain Picard in the *Star Trek: The Next Generation* series, recently pointed me to a really interesting post in the *McKinsey Quarterly* titled "Leadership Lessons from the Royal Navy."

Now, I'd not really want to serve in Nelson's navy or occupy a gun turret on a World War I dreadnought, but the Royal Navy has had a certain luster (or lustre, I guess) for a long, long time, and its greatest leaders—Nelson and Jellicoe, for example—have something to teach us.

The McKinsey piece, by Andrew St. George, explores a few aspects of the culture that has made the British navy a formidable and storied fighting force since the sixteenth century.

One factor in creating the Royal Navy's positive culture with strong values around authentic communication is the encouragement of banter—easy conversational give-and-take, often humorous or teasing, a game of verbal badminton that often weaves together the superficial and the essential. The British style of banter has long crossed frontiers of class and rank, not transgressively but rather in a way that creates a path for the transmission of important information when needed. Writes St. George, in the Royal Navy "the practice of 'banter'… is … openly encouraged as an upbeat and informal way to regulate relationships and break down hierarchy. Banter occurs at all ranks and quite often between them. A Royal Navy driver will talk more readily to a Second Sea Lord than the average corporate employee will engage his or her CEO in an elevator."

Banter of one sort or another tends to characterize life in schools. As adults we probably don't hear about ninety percent of student banter, and of course we know that student banter can escalate into or sometimes mask—in an ugly and perniciously subtle way—teasing that is truly unkind, and even outright bullying.

But we can model and encourage "good" banter—the kind that eases the strains in relationships and helps students learn the critical skill of talking to adults—by practicing and nurturing it in our classrooms, lunch tables, hallways, and dormitories and indeed by making it the hallmark of our most effective relationships with students. Banter can be used to gently redirect or focus a student whose actions have taken a wrong turn, and it can be used to reinforce and praise without quite awkwardly laying on laurels. Banter can be used to jolly students toward new understandings and insight—and students bantering with us can push us in all these same directions.

In the summers of my younger days I worked on the food service and buildings and grounds crews of a number of different institutions—schools, colleges, and youth service agencies. A somewhat shy kid, I had grown up around adults who were by and large intellectual and awfully serious, but in these less academic environments I learned about banter, the joshing and cajoling and occasional flashes of purposeful sarcasm used by the grown-ups on these crews to process and occasionally defuse aspects of their workday lives. Often enough, the endless and often clever banter just made more interesting, bearable, and even fun the repetitive and not always super-stimulating work of, say, preparing two hundred servings of baked chicken, building a new sidewalk, or edging eighteen holes' worth of sand traps. The banter made work enjoyable, lightening tasks and building relationships among the crewmembers that really did cross boundaries of age, race, and social class.

I remember one young and stern boss, whose seriousness and idiosyncrasies quickly became fodder for a great deal of banter among us behind his back. At some point one of the veterans ventured to direct right at the boss a gentle tease; we all froze, waiting for a harsh response.

Instead, the boss teased back, acknowledging his own quirkiness on this particular subject, and from that point forward the whole crew became more relaxed and productive—and the boss, having acknowledged a certain vulnerability but now engaging with the crew as peers on a shared mission (just in different roles), became much more confident and even easy-going.

As I play back the mental tapes of impressions and memory from my years in schools, I can attest to the fact that many of the most effective teachers I have ever had or worked with were inveterate banterers, whose easy and yet gently and positively provocative conversations with students were the locus of much of their best work.

These teachers also made great colleagues, whose humor and generally upbeat approach to life invited colleagues into a positive space, sometimes working subtexts that nudged the rest of us toward exploring new perspectives and approaches to our practice or helped build consensus around particular points of view on school policy.

School culture, then, is every bit as subject to and in need of the effects of vigorous, openhearted banter as the Royal Navy. As small communities striving to knit themselves into a cohesive unit, except in purpose not so unlike a naval vessel, schools need to foster just the kinds of easy, open, and positive cultures that St. George claims banter helps create in the British Navy.

Any of Admiral Horatio Nelson's cadre of young captains—the Band of Brothers whose victory at Trafalgar the Royal Navy views as its finest hour—would happily have taken the bullet that killed their commander in that battle, and the record suggests that their open and easy relationships with one another—at meals, off duty, and sometimes on deck—were a part of the reason. The love they bore for Nelson was greatly inspired by his own willingness to be himself among them, not unlike the good attitude that made my own young boss so successful in the end. One suspects that this openness was paradoxically not a small source of the confidence that made Nelson such a decisive, clear-headed leader; he knew he didn't have to impress anyone, just organize and inspire them.

This also makes me reflect on how the benefits of banter may be transferred to digital environments, where the nuances of tone and pitch that so often characterize face-to-face banter may be lost, or reduced to the paltry explanatory power of emoticons. In my experience banter moves faster than my fingers can type. But I guess I do engage in banter-esque discourse via text and even email, and I can imagine that for digital natives e-banter is probably as easy and common as it was at the dinner table in Nelson's cabin aboard HMS *Victory*.

So, as you wander the halls of your school and poke your head into its classrooms, be alert for banter, and consider its power. If you're a leader, consider how your own willingness to engage in banter—with everyone in your school—might support not just your relationships but the strategic work you must organize and inspire. It might not be Trafalgar, but it is about improving the lives of the children in your care.

Not Your Father's School, February 3, 2013

47 JOB DESCRIPTIONS

Periodically one or another of the independent school teaching listservs and networks will light up with queries about job descriptions. Sometimes these are quite specific; someone at a school will want to know about the title and responsibilities of his or her counterparts at other schools. Occasionally the queries are about structure, accountability, and reporting status.

About once a year, however, the question is more general, relating to the nature of a "full-time job" description—how many classes, how many students, how many hours, how many extracurricular responsibilities? The inquirer may have been commissioned to survey the field, or perhaps they taking it upon themself to find answers.

Those who have been through a full-blown discussion of this at their own schools will recognize in the question a generalized anxiety that goes well beyond "job descriptions." No one asks this question out of idle curiosity; there is almost always something deeper, and more difficult, at stake.

Working from a fairly small sample of schools I've worked in, colleagues' schools, and schools where I've been asked to speak about professional culture, my observation is that these discussions grow out of a certain sense or undefined worry that responsibilities and rewards are not evenly distributed. Often, it seems that conversations about these issues arise fairly early in a time of institutional transition: a change of leadership, the announcement of a new initiative, or a sudden economic downturn.

Even the most carefully managed and comprehensible changes in many schools create uncertainty. Whether teachers are inherently skittish and conservative or whether the traditional isolation of classroom teaching creates its own kind of solipsistic anxiety—I tend to favor the latter explanation—teachers, like cubicle dwellers or prairie dogs (the comparison has been around for a while), react to the winds of change by popping their heads up and nervously sniffing the air to assess their own situation vis-á-vis their peers.

Concern in the face of change is not unreasonable. Will the new leaders appreciate me? Will they favor someone else? Will they understand what I do, and why? Will they recognize and reward my work as has been done in the past? Will I be able to adapt and fit into the new kind of work I am being asked to do? Will my position survive in hard times?

What begins as individual concern, however, can snowball into something corrosive in the presence of more serious concerns. Has the previous administration played favorites in a way that is likely to be undone or—worse—sustained by the new arrivals? Are there unspoken rivalries and resentments within the school community—between divisions, or departments, for example—that have people suddenly asking those "will I be valued?" questions in terms of "them versus us"? Are there real or imagined systemic inequities that are part of the shared experience of the teaching faculty? Are there programs or positions that don't appear to justify their existence as programmatic "value added"?

The change, whatever its nature, thus creates an environment in which faculties may display some of their least admirable traits: mistrust, self-protection, and resistance. Even with relatively cool and rational teacher-leaders in the vanguard, the pressure to explore "job descriptions" in an atmosphere of fear or mistrust is generally too strong to be resisted, and thus the queries begin.

Of course, the real question at the heart of the matter is, *Are all teachers at our school acknowledged and valued equally for the hard work they have been doing, and will equity be a hallmark of the new regime or new system?* Corollaries include, *Will existing areas of relative unfairness be corrected?* and, *Is my continued employment, assuming I continue to do all that I am asked to do, going to be assured?*

For administrators, these conversations, vexing and acrimonious as they can be, should be regarded as golden opportunities to respond to teachers' concerns proactively. If salaries and their determination have historically been a mystery or a closely guarded secret, there might never be a better time to engage faculty in developing a scale of some sort. If a new administration discovers inequities, a rapid effort to remedy these will be much appreciated. If a new initiative might conceivably have serious repercussions for some teachers, then serious efforts must be made to mitigate these where possible, perhaps through professional development, or at least to make clear the real nature of the issue. If tough times may indeed force cutbacks, make clear the risks and the ways in which staff reductions will be determined.

The trick, I think, is for administrators to help faculties get beyond issues like class loads and minutes spent leading clubs or coaching teams. I like to think that at most schools, and certainly virtually all good and happy ones, there is essentially just one "job description": teachers arrive in the morning, work hard all day in the service of students and the school's mission, and go home in the evening, even when home is a dormitory; dorm work is part of the job description for many independent school teachers, and they are compensated for this work in some way.

Good and happy schools make certain that equal contribution is rewarded by equal compensation. (Schools are not rich, and sometimes the coin of the realm in faculty compensation is not take-home cash but rather benefits—housing, insurance, and even time.)

I would observe here that there is a slippery slope for schools in the establishment of compensation programs that use elaborate systems of points or stipends to "reward" teachers. Along with headaches for those charged with managing such systems, they also create and enshrine invidious comparisons. My suspicion is that not a few of such programs were born of "job description" kerfuffles in times of institutional stress or change. Whether there is a way to reel them in to be replaced by more globally based systems, I do not know, but I think it would be hard, even if the end result would be a more congenial professional culture.

In 2007 NAIS undertook a survey on teacher satisfaction. In the results there was a strong correlation in the areas of both compensation and professional culture that is based on a few basic things that make teachers happy. Key factors, not surprisingly, are

- ✓ Transparency in decision-making
- ✓ Involvement of teachers in both general decision-making and the design of compensation and benefit programs

- ✓ Clear communication within the school, including of course but not limited to that between administration and teachers
- ✓ Visibility of the school's leadership in the professional world of faculty members
- ✓ Recognition and appreciation of effective work
- ✓ Opportunities for authentic growth

Administrators focused on creating or maintaining the "good and happy school" to which I have made reference understand these matters, and not just in the abstract.

Such a school will already have in place a clear and consistently applied system of professional evaluation based on clear and well understood standards for effective teaching. It will be clear and consistent in the way that decisions are made and communicated, and there will be great opportunities for all teachers to learn and grow as professionals and as adults. Everyone will appreciate the efforts of everyone else and understand that each colleague, peer and administrator alike, is doing their best work, all the time, in a positive and productive atmosphere.

It's not about job descriptions, but about the work.
Admirable Faculties, November 16, 2008

48 PARENT-TEACHER EVENTS

It's time again for parent conferences, parent evenings, back-to-school nights, and all the rich variety of ways that schools devise to bring families into schools to build important connections and begin essential conversations (as Sara Lawrence-Lightfoot has so aptly called them) between teachers and parent/guardians.

As much as anything, parents and guardians want to be reassured that their children are in good, caring hands and that their children are doing what is necessary to be successful in school. For schools, the time is right to make sure that teachers are confident and comfortable either sitting down with individual parents or standing up to explain what they do to a room full of them.

For new teachers, especially, these events can be nerve-wracking, and so it is the job of department and division leaders and mentors to work with new teachers to develop successful approaches or even something like scripts. For class presentations, the teacher should be ready to introduce himself or herself, to discuss the aims of the course, and to model in some way the classroom culture that the students experience. The "Be yourself" advice that is true for facing a classroom of students is every bit as true when the desks are occupied by curious parents. Some teachers will want to try a class-like exercise, but this should be simple, contained in its aims, and clearly connected with the purposes of the class. As parents we have noticed that these events don't always provide opportunities to establish relationships with our children's classmates' families, and a clever teacher might even integrate some "getting to know you" elements.

For conferences, teachers need to prepare themselves by having anecdotal and specific information about each student; what families want to know most is that a teacher knows and cares about their child. The point is to talk about the child, so the focus should be on aspects of behavior and performance and not just on grades—I always advise keeping the gradebook off to the side, closed but bookmarked, and not in front of me like a sacred text. Teachers should not be afraid to ask questions: "How does the student talk about the class at home?", "What are the student's interests?", and "What are your concerns?" can yield really valuable answers. Above all, the teacher should have some positive things to say, observations of strengths as well as areas for improvement. Behavioral concerns should not be whitewashed, but they should be presented based on anecdote and not as labels or judgments. Teachers must be careful about either dragging other students' behavior into the conversation or about shooting themselves in the foot by alluding to general problems in the classroom. Good teachers understand that children of particular ages will have particular foibles and refer to these not as character flaws but as developmental issues to be acknowledged and dealt with as part of helping the student grow up.

Teachers almost always dread events involving parents, but in my experience such things almost always go well; parents genuinely appreciate caring teachers and precise, well-intentioned feedback that they can use to support their children in finding success in school. There are always a few parents who in the course of their children's education will feel the need to launch a zinger question or comment at a teacher, but the best deflection is either a bland "I think that's a great question [because often it is, even if framed unpleasantly], and it's something we think about quite often" or to suggest a separate conversation at a later time. (I once innocently asked such a question of my spouse when I sat as a parent in her classroom, assuming that I had pitched her a beachball that she would hit out of the park, but the way I phrased it so flustered her that I am still ruing that moment six years later.)

The economic turmoil in this autumn of 2008 will be having an unsettling effect on families, and so there may be some new symptoms of parental anxiety around the very appropriate but usually unspoken question, "Is the money we are spending on independent school worth it?" The best answer is not so much a specific cost-benefit analysis but rather what I would call a cultural response by the school and all of its teachers. Families are paying the long dollar to have their children challenged, nourished, prepared, and above all cared for as individuals. Parent–teacher events are the ideal opportunities to showcase the depth of the school's collective affection and concern for its students, and above all, teachers should understand this and see this as a primary goal of these occasions.

In troubled times, especially, using family–teacher events for sharing both positive feelings and well-meaning concerns about students can be extremely comforting for both families and faculties. We all found that to be true in the anguished September of 2001, and it will be no less so now, and so let us enter the season of such events in a spirit of positive anticipation and mutual support.

Admirable Faculties, September 30, 2008

49   HOLIDAY GREETINGS: FAMILY STYLE!

Lamarck may have had it wrong—critters don't evolve on demand—but I'm always amazed at the speed with which certain things can become so ingrained in our consciousness as to constitute a kind of species memory. Vast tracts of my brain are devoted to old advertising slogans, songs I didn't care for very much, character names from sitcoms long forgotten, and images; I'm never surprised when others of my vintage can produce or at least recognize the same mental detritus of times past.

It's the images that are often embedded most firmly, and probably few artists have done as much to both capture and then concretize these as eternal cultural iconography as Norman Rockwell. Rockwell gave our holidays, especially, a kind of sheen and even substance that we have a hard time sloughing off.

I dare you to close your eyes and imagine a holiday dinner table—roast something, multiple generations, heaping helpings, eager faces—without seeing it somehow as limned by Rockwell, with bright colors, odd details, happy and hungry grins. In some way our holiday dinners are all striving to be, well, Rockwellesque: life imitating art.

Over the past several months I have had occasion to experience at a number of so-called "junior boarding schools" something almost forgotten at many day schools: sit-down, family-style meals. Rather than the free-fire zone of cafeteria lines and unrestrained boisterousness of student-only seating, I've sat patiently while student waiters brought trays of food to be served out by teachers at tables where something like old-fashioned, or even Rockwellesque decorum prevails (complete with odd details and happy grins, mind you; these are kids).

For one accustomed to a faster, louder school dining experience, family-style meals are at first quaint, then a pleasant contrast, and at last wondrous. Conversations can occur; food is apportioned according to the number of people at the table, not the immediate desire of each hungry individual. Seconds are available. Salt (and pepper!) are passed upon request, napkins go immediately to laps, and what my mother always called the "boarding house reach" is expressly discouraged.

At such meals I've learned a great deal about the other people—students and teachers alike—at the table, and I've eaten my fill, too. I haven't noted any absence of joy or exuberance, just an absence of excess noise and questionable manners. I've also enjoyed the mixed-ness of ages, grade levels, and perspectives, qualities generally lost in the clique-y homogenization of cafeteria lunch tables. Each meal is an exercise in the power of banter, a little workshop in social and emotional learning.

The other day I heard on NPR a piece on school lunches and the ever-declining amounts of time kids in many schools (mostly public, but that was the focus of the segment) have to eat them, and the crowded and rushed conditions under which many kids have to eat. The whole nutrition question, it seems to me, is mooted when "speed eating" is the order of the day. Listening made me appreciate even more the joys of family-style meals.

When my extended family sits down together in a few days we'll all be privately aspiring to achieve Rockwellesque-ness, and I will regret for a few moments at least that the eating experiences that most schools provide students aren't a bit more this way on a regular basis.

This may just read as the sad ramblings of an old man from a bygone era; family-style meals aren't going to make a comeback in schools, and I should get over it. But where this tradition persists, kids and adults share something every day that the rest of us will find ourselves yearning for as we gather ceremonially with family and friends to tuck into our roast beast. It probably doesn't matter much in the great scale of things, but I'm a fan.

I'm also a fan of relaxation and taking pleasure in both leisure and the company of loved ones. If I could invite all readers to a holiday feast (served family-style!) at Not Your Father's School, I would; but since I cannot, I herewith pass along all my best seasonal wishes to you and to ours.

Not Your Father's School, December 22, 2013

ESPECIALLY FOR INDEPENDENT SCHOOL TEACHERS

Perspective by John Gulla, *Executive Director, Edward E. Ford Foundation*:
I experienced an epiphany some 30 years ago when I first read *The Call of Stories* by Robert Coles. I thought of my childhood years in an Italian-Irish Catholic family outside of Boston and the parables I heard every Sunday in church. I thought of my own teachers and coaches and mentors in elementary and secondary school and in college and graduate school. Who and what did I remember and why? Of those who helped teach me what I then knew, how did they best do so? The most memorable and effective teaching is often storytelling. Peter Gow is a life-long teacher and storyteller, as you'll soon read in these collected pieces.

Over the last half dozen years, Peter and I have had a number of exchanges that have shown me that the 1960s idealism that pulled Peter to the family trade and committed him to a thoughtful life as a teacher has annealed over the course of his career and matured as a result of his experience into some of the wisdom you will find here. I feel, as Peter might—I'll have to ask him—that a life spent around teenagers inspires hopefulness that decades in schools can sometimes temper. But not in Peter Gow. I read what he writes and often agree and sometimes push against, but I rarely click away. He tells me stories, and I'm not bored.

As the son of two public school teachers and the nephew of a dozen more, I know of the public/independent school divide that can inform some discussions of the two worlds. For longer and more effectively than most, Peter has built bridges between these two worlds. For all of his interests in curriculum, equity and justice, college admission, technology and more, he has never lost the focus that good work in this world must always be about teaching. He has a lifetime to stories about teaching to tell us.

50 I AM AN INDEPENDENT SCHOOL TEACHER—WHY?

I started teaching in 1974, defaulting to what I knew: the tiny boarding school founded by my grandfather and at that time headed by my uncle. After a year and a half a personal matter—love, if you have to ask—found me in yet another independent school, where for three years I honed my craft under great mentors.

A child of the Sixties, I graduated from high school—yes, an independent school—in 1968 and experienced college amid protests and draft worries, resenting the hidden powers behind the status quo. By 1976 I had cut my hair, but I still had dreams of a more egalitarian world, and so that year I began the coursework toward public school certification.

People often speak deploringly of ed courses, but mine (at Rhode Island College and the University of Rhode Island) were well taught and filled with engaged students. I discovered that teaching was something that people thought about and even researched. I think I became a better, or at least more intentional, teacher.

Alas, as I was finishing two things occurred. One, I became a parent and more risk-averse about changing jobs, and two, big cuts to public education had begun—think Prop Two-and-a-Half in Massachusetts and California Proposition 13. Instead of hiring, districts in New England were firing. It was the era of RIF: reduction in force.

Thirty-some years later, I am still in an independent school. My current place looks much like the real world of Boston and its suburbs: no uniforms or ties, not much paneling on the walls. Kids ride in on the train, in parents' work vans, and (yes) in brand-new luxury SUVs. There's an application process, and tuition is high, but a quarter of our kids receive financial aid, much of it in large amounts. We have students who can attend because their parents work extra jobs; plenty of our parents struggle to find time for school functions.

It's not the same as public school, I know. My democratizing instincts were blunted, you could claim, and now I suppose I can be viewed as "the other." But I am confident that I am in a place whose kids aren't all that different from most of those at suburban high schools around the country. They do homework, play sports, hang out with friends, play video games—what kids do. Yes, they will all attend college, but more than you might imagine will receive need-based financial aid for this.

The good news, for me, is that our school turns out more than our fair share of teachers, entrepreneurs, artists, and social issue advocates. Our graduates hold onto the values we try to realize in our daily work: that people matter more than money, that being creative and being yourself matter more than living up to someone else's idea of what you are supposed to be. These values keep me around.

Plenty of other people in independent schools—leaders, teachers, coaches, even trustees—share similar values and daily experiences. We are not fleeing or countering public education but simply part of a choice someone has made for our students. Whether the opportunity to make this choice represents a flaw in our society I cannot say, but I don't happen to think so. Students enroll, and someone needs to teach them. I'm lucky to do this in an environment consonant with my ideals.

Independent schools aren't better than public schools, just different. And we teachers all got into this business because we believe in kids, and because we want to give kids a good shot at a happy, successful adulthood. Maybe it's easier to do this where I am, but it's never been that easy, for example, for the teachers of the dyslexic students whose struggles inspired my grandfather to start his own independent school in 1926. These teachers still work their heads off, just as their students do. So, I hasten to add, do all the public-school teachers I know.

I'm often write in hopes of dispelling some of the myths and stereotypes around what I do and to better understand other sectors. I want to share ideas and stories and explore how we might have a dialogue and even work in partnership. I want to hear about what public schools can teach us.

Mostly, I just want to reinforce what I believe from the bottom of my heart: whether we work in public schools, religious schools, charter schools, or independent schools, we and our students and our society are all in this together.

"Independent Schools, Common Perspectives," *Education Week*, February 17, 2013

51 SOME THOUGHTS AND RESOURCES ON INDEPENDENT SCHOOL TEACHING

About ten years back, based on an article I had written for Independent School magazine, I was asked by the National Association of Independent Schools to put together a proposal for a book on hiring, training, and retaining teachers. *An Admirable Faculty: Recruiting, Hiring, Training, and Retaining the Best Independent School Teachers* appeared in 2005, and I stand by the content, dated as some of it may be.

The themes of *An Admirable Faculty* seemed to resonate still as I have tracked the Twitter stream and some the compelling Storifies and blog posts emerging from the NAIS Science of Learning and 21st Century Schools Summit at Vanderbilt University recently. The technology may have advanced, but I don't think it has become any less important for schools to be developing:

- ✓ truly thoughtful mission- and culture-informed recruiting and hiring campaigns (not just "dial-an-agency" hiring)
- ✓ equally thoughtful induction programs for new faculty focusing on expectations, school culture, and a

- schools' unique approaches or methods comprehensive mentoring programs for all early-career teachers
- ✓ menus of rich professional development opportunities built around both the needs and capacities of each teacher and the strategic needs and capacities of the school
- ✓ an articulated set of school-based standards for what it means to be an effective teacher—in all a teacher's roles, and
- ✓ thoughtful management and encouragement of faculty career paths, including leadership opportunities and development and ways of tapping the developed skills of master teachers.

In fact, I was so committed to the ideas of thoughtful and "intentional" that a few years later I wrote a book for teachers and prospective teachers that was kind of the mirror of *An Admirable Faculty*. Called *The Intentional Teacher: Forging a Great Career in the Independent School Classroom* (Avocus, 2009), the book offers teachers basic advice on the carrying out various responsibilities of an independent teacher at all levels and in all kids of schools, of course including classroom teaching. (On this topic, among the better advice is to acquire and read Jon Saphier's *The Skillful Teacher*, co-authored by Mary Ann Haley-Speca and Robert Gower and published by his Research for Better Teaching organization; it's the best one-stop shopping handbook for building classroom skills that I have found.)

Again, technology has advanced, but I like to think that *The Intentional Teacher*'s "inside" thoughts on what that "great career" might look are still relevant. I feel the same way about its advice on taking institutional responsibilities into one's own hands if they are not offered by the school—how to be a mentor, how to help colleagues manage their own careers, how to imagine one's own "standards" for effective professionalism. There are other outstanding resources on great teaching—Harry and Rosemary Wong's *The First Days of School: How to Be an Effective Teacher*, Doug Lemov's *Teach Like a Champion*—but as far as I know there aren't a lot of books besides a handful in the Avocus list that pertain directly to independent school teaching and teacher-leadership. (It's worth mentioning that Carolyn Kost's *Engage! Setting the Course for Independent Secondary Schools in the 21st Century* includes many excellent thoughts on the transformation of teaching.)

I read the NAIS Summit at Vanderbilt as a clear signal that the Association is interested in advancing teaching and learning and in supporting teachers. I'm personally excited about this because it aligns with what is obviously a great personal passion. Post-books, I started blogging, and I have tried to sustain teaching themes at *Admirable Faculties* for some years and now here at *Not Your Father's School*.

Best of all, the Summit has stoked anew the critical conversation on what it means to be an effective independent school teacher and what it looks like for a school as a whole to offer a program that is delivered skillfully, intentionally, and effectively. The framework of independent school education still demands empathetic, knowledgeable, and creative teachers, but the elements of the work we do in and out of the classroom are evolving rapidly and continuously. New books and new blog posts will in time be written to explore possibilities yet unimagined—exciting times!

To ice this post's self-promotional cake, I'd also invite those interested in the advancement of independent school cultures and practices in teaching and learning to stay tuned to the growing body of offerings developed by the Independent Curriculum Group [and now, in 2020, supported and being expanded by One Schoolhouse]. We're dedicated to supporting schools and teachers in developing their capacities in pedagogy, curriculum, and assessment with a focus on what works for students within the culture of their own schools.

Not Your Father's School, May 21, 2015

52 INDEPENDENT SCHOOLS, INDEPENDENT TEACHERS: FREEDOM AND RESPONSIBILITY

The other day a discussion thread appeared on the National Association of Independent Schools online communities speculating on aspects of the great freedom that independent school teachers have to create curriculum and assessments suited to their strengths and to the particular needs and interests of their students and their schools. This got me to thinking.

This freedom has long been a classic double-edged sword. The virtues of "teacher autonomy" in independent schools were extolled to me even before I entered the field back in the Nixon era. As another veteran of that era has commented to me, the idea long prevailed in many schools (and perhaps still does in some) that a teacher would be taken to the door to the classroom, handed a textbook (a.k.a. the "curriculum"), and assured that paychecks would clear until June, short of some act that would rate firing for cause. What happened in the classroom would, by some sort of gentleman's agreement, stay in the classroom, and the teacher would not be inconvenienced by, say, a rigorous evaluation process.

I know that this was once true, because I experienced it. In retrospect it makes me angrier every time I think about it, angrier that I had a couple of years (at least) when no one other than my students offered me feedback that might have made me a better teacher. Except for casual bull sessions with colleagues and occasional soul-baring to my spouse, I missed out on informed discussions on how I might have created a richer classroom culture, designed a more engaging curriculum, come up with better ways of measuring student performance, or been an even more engaged monitor and mentor to my students. I muddled through, believing I was improving, and I probably was—but still. Steve Clem, late of the Association of Independent Schools of New England and a passionate exponent of teacher feedback, shares a similar story, and similar vexation, as part of his workshops on classroom observation and feedback.

Things are generally better now. Each new iteration of school accreditation standards has raised the bar for what constitutes effective and comprehensive supervision and evaluation in independent schools, and better still, conversations about teaching and learning are becoming more widespread in the professional cultures at many, if not most, independent schools.

"Professional development," once a suspect term, has become A Good Thing, generally, and the majority of teachers have seen in the changing landscape of pedagogy and curriculum design both opportunities and responsibilities to improve their craft. Catching up with our public school counterparts, lots of independent schools talk about creating professional cultures, even professional learning communities or "communities of practice." It's about damn time, and there has been mercifully little accompanying talk of "value-added" models.

Some years ago I became involved in the Independent Curriculum Group (ICG), a consortium of schools wanting to engage in conversations about school-based, teacher-created curriculum and to support the idea that teaching to someone else's test isn't necessary the most effective use of the skills and energies of an able, creative faculty. The ICG, with a handful of public and charter schools among its members, facilitated these conversations for a few years. Rather than being about "autonomy," the ICG was about the responsibility that schools and teachers have to design work based on student needs and institutional values and aims and that elicits from students both real engagement and authentic, challenging learning.

So when I think of freedom, independent school-style, I think not of total "liberation in your classroom" but rather of the serious, lifelong obligation all teachers have to keep improving their work in the service of the kids in their classrooms. Freedom we have, but like any kind of freedom, it comes with serious responsibility that teachers and schools must embrace.

"Independent Schools, Common Perspectives," *Education Week*, February 19, 2013

THE EPILOGUES

Perspective by Catherine Conover, *Development Officer at Vassar College and long-time college and university administrator*
Those who know Peter Gow far better than I and those who have been reading his reflections on education over the years know he has a way with words and the ability to distill big ideas into very digestible morsels. Still, writing something about someone you know intimately that has relevance and strikes a chord with those who did know him/her well is a real gift. In these two essays Peter reflects on the careers of his father and his wife, two devoted teachers as unalike in most respects as any two people might ever be. In each essay he captures the nature of what made them memorable but also shines a light on the institutions at which they worked and the lasting impact of the work they did. No teacher could ask for a better epitaph. We can hope each will, in their time, receive one as good.

PG note, 2020: *It is a sad fact of life that too often we reflect on teaching and the nature of great teachers only as we memorialize them. My father taught for his whole working life, retired at 66, and spent the last two decades of his life missing the classroom. My late spouse discovered her desire to teach in her late twenties, earned a teaching degree, and spent the next thirty years in the classroom. I share here, as a kind of coda to this book, posts I wrote subsequent to their deaths.*

53   THE LAST POST FOR MY FATHER

We've become accustomed to the moving spectacle of funerals of firefighters and police officers, where comrades from many jurisdictions show the colors, ride in formation, and remind us by their solidarity of the perilous and valuable work they do. Since September 11 of 2001, these events are even more emotionally gripping, more significant as reminders of the fragility of life and the weird and unpredictable forces at work in nature as well as humankind.

Of course, we don't expect such for teachers, and anyhow in the education sector we don't much tend toward uniforms (tweeds for men, colorful scarves for women?) and flags. But my father's memorial service the other day was as close as I expect ever to come to one of those funerals, and it brought me strangely face to face with some aspects of this work than I have been reflecting on.

First, there were scores of my father's old students, some of whom had also been my grandfather's—men who had been in the classrooms at my father's school sixty years ago and more. A line my siblings and I became accustomed to hearing that day was, "You know, your dad (or your grandfather) saved my life."

These men are dyslexic and make no bones about it. The realization that they had a learning disability was the first step toward building lives that weren't going to be defined by the deficiency labels that peers, family members, and (I regret to say) even teachers were delighted to put on dyslexic kids in an earlier day: "stupid," "lazy," "uneducable"—even, heaven help us, "retarded." Gow School students past and present unanimously recount their relief when they realized that everyone else in their classes had the same challenges, and they can still—all these years later—recite some of the strategies they applied as they learned to compensate for their dyslexia.

And they remain grateful, perhaps extravagantly but I think not, for the "life-saving" education they received. They're doctors, lawyers, writers, filmmakers, entrepreneurs—doing all the work that able, educated adults can do. And they see their education, and their teachers, as having rescued them from lives less focused, less satisfying—the frustrated lives of good minds limited in scope and cut off from opportunities by a learning disability.

So, a theme of the day was life-saving. I was never so proud.

But there was a second, more surprising thing, something I could have anticipated but that thirty-seven years of living in what we jokingly call the "Buffalo diaspora" had pushed from my mind. There was a kind of parade of figures from my own educational past: the wonderful high school math teacher who came into my life too late to save me from a life of uncertainty when faced with problems more complex than Algebra I; my fourth-grade teacher (imagine!), the only male classroom teacher at the suburban elementary school to which I had traveled each day from our tiny village and later the principal of the new elementary school (now closed) to which my younger brothers had gone; a host of former teachers from Gow whom I had known before, during, and after my own year-and-a-half as a teacher there; a high school classmate and close friend—my own supportive wingman when my grandmother had died in her home across the street from mine when I was a senior in high school.

My classmate's own dad had been my seventh-grade English teacher and the man who had suggested I start reading the sports pages and the comics so as to be able to actually converse with real people; I was apparently a bit abstracted from the agony and sweat of the human spirit in junior high. His son, my friend, now in turn teaches writing to people of all ages and has achieved what was once my dream of being a regular columnist, wry and funny and engaged and generous in his love for his community, for the local weekly newspaper—a mentor not just to his students but to his town. (Check out [this collection of his work](#) or the archives of "The View from Right Field" in the *East Aurora Advertiser*, if you're a fan of this estimable branch of journalism.)

These teacherly types and former, appreciative students made concrete for me something I already vaguely suspected: that teachers belong to their students at least as much as to their families. The best and most confident teachers are truly themselves in their classrooms perhaps as nowhere else, and so their students see them and know them intimately and have the opportunity to understand them—and to care for them if the right chemistry is at work—better, perhaps, than their own households.

It's comforting, then, and kind of awe-inspiring to know that memories of my father will stay not just with my immediate family but with the thousand men he taught. Even if there weren't uniforms (if you don't count the school blazers that the current head and a few current students were wearing and the tartan tie sported by one of my nephews), the feeling was there—that we were saying goodbye to a guy who had saved lives, and that we were well supported by our own kind, sharing as teachers do our peculiar understanding of the weird and unpredictable forces at work in our own quiet and pretty humble profession.

I hate to add a political note, but I couldn't help wishing that all the politicians who have been bashing teachers lately could have been there.

Not Your Father's School, December 15, 2011

54   ON THE DEATH OF A TEACHER

For the last week my attention has been held by a sad and personal situation involving our worst nightmare: the death of a teacher, an active, working teacher. She said good-bye to her fifth-grade students in the carpool line on a Friday, hale and hearty, and by midnight on Saturday she was gone, suddenly and unexpectedly.

Grief specialists tell us to use the hard words in these situations and avoid euphemisms, especially when we are speaking with children. They can provide our institutions with scripts and protocols for managing the first flush of shock and sadness, and schools that have experienced the death of a current student or teacher learn how important it is to develop—just about instantly—strategies for helping members of the community cope with the initial emotional devastation, felt in a different way by each teacher, student, and staff member.

In this case the school handled the situation beautifully, with full and swift communication within the community and special outreach to the graduating classes, students and parents/guardians alike, of the teacher's children, who had both attended the school. Those who needed to know and who would most have wanted to know were informed quickly and fully. As it turned out, the family had already reached out to the school about hosting a memorial event, and so critical connections had been initiated.

Of course, special attention was lavished on the teacher's students and immediate colleagues, including her teaching partner of 15 years. There was time to process the initial shock—it's the only word, and so it must be repeated—and to surface both anxieties and happy memories. For the whole day, which happened to be October 31, the schedule of events had been shifted to permit grieving, recollection, and the first steps toward memorial and celebration—and still allow students to embrace the fun of Halloween.

This past Wednesday evening there was a memorial event in the packed school gymnasium. The school community, along with other circles of which the teacher had been a part, came together for a moving and beautiful tribute featuring shared memories from family members, colleagues, and friends. Her children inspired the room, but most affecting were her students recalling their teacher's passion for sharing her love of doing the work of the mind, especially reading; there was the "Harry Potter Challenge," where the teacher would bake chocolate chip cookies for any student who completed the first book in the series. Said one little girl, "I'm dyslexic. I used to hate reading. Then my teacher got me to read *Harry Potter*, and now I love reading and I'll always remember her."

It was hard to suppress the thought that this lavish display of affection, admiration, and just plain love was coming just a bit too late, at least for the teacher. But this is the way of memorials; at best we can hope that the teacher died with an inkling of the place she occupied in people's hearts and the influence she had on a generation and more of students, and those who knew her best believe that she did.

But even more apparent was what this event, sparked by what might qualify as a tragedy, meant for the school. It's barely November, still relatively early in a new school year, and there's a new head of school. In a way, the death of a teacher is a test of a school's character: How well can the community recover its emotional center and remind itself of its core values? On Wednesday night this school came together, rediscovered its heart, and affirmed its long-established capacity for unqualified love.

I happened to have been married to this teacher. I thought I'd seen just about everything in the school biz, but it turns out I hadn't. The gift of seeing how much she mattered to so many other people can't compensate for her loss, but it's quite a wonderful thing. Feeling her school grieve with me, watching their own struggle toward healing, is helping me and our kids heal, too. We're all of us school folk, and I guess we instinctively look to schools for what we need. This past week we have been finding it. A schoolteacher she was, and she teaches still.

The Independent Curriculum Group Newsletter, November 2016

www.ingramcontent.com/pod-product-compliance
Lightning Source LLC
Chambersburg PA
CBHW022114040426
42450CB00006B/700